Albert Einstein:

The Biography of a Genius Who Changed Science and World History

Born: March 14, 1879

Died: April 18, 1955

Respective authors own all copyrights not held by the publisher.

The information herein is offered for informational purposes only, and is universal as so. The presentation of the information is without contract or any type of guarantee assurance.

The trademarks are used without consent, and the publication of the trademark is without permission or backing by the trademark owner. All trademarks and brands within this book are for clarification purposes only and are owned by the owners themselves and not affiliated with this document.

ISBN 978-1-9992202-8-0

Published by Pluto King Publishing

Table of Contents

Chapter 25: Einstein's Scientific Achievements

257

Chapter 26: Other Major Achievements   **267**

Chapter 27: Various Proofs of the Validity of Einstein's Laws   277

Chapter 28: Einstein's Life Away from Physics   285

Chapter 29: Einstein's Prolific Scientific Journey   295

Introductory Note

Dear Reader,

Thank you for purchasing this book.

This book provides a detailed account of Einstein's life, including his personal life as well as his achievements.

I hope you will benefit from this book.

If it does bring you enjoyment, would you be kind enough to leave a positive review on Amazon? I would greatly appreciate it.

Thanks again.

Chapter 1: Early Life

The genius who indirectly helped to create the atomic bomb, Albert Einstein, was born on March 14, 1879. While his early childhood was unimpressive, Einstein later earned the respect of the entire world and won the coveted Nobel Prize. His name is the most revered in physics. Even though he was a well-respected genius, Einstein mingled freely among ordinary folk, just as easily as he did scholars and politicians. And while Einstein had a great sense of humor, he was also a bit reckless in the way he led his personal life.

To truly appreciate this brilliant scientist, who, at the age of 26, wrote the scholarly articles that fundamentally altered the foundation of physics, it is first important to look at his background and the environment in which he grew up in. Interestingly, while Einstein's performance in math and physics was outstanding, he was not the only one in his family with a brilliant mind. His father also had an inclination towards mathematics, and his sister earned a doctorate in literature.

Closest Family

Born into a Jewish family, Einstein never became a practicing Jew. This is not to say that he was averse to religion. As discussed later, in his work, Einstein, in fact, made an effort to link religion to science and vice-versa, later expressing his conviction that neither could do without the other. Eventually, he did develop an interest in Judaism.

Father

Einstein's father, Hermann Einstein, was born in 1847, and was a man of German-Jewish decent, whose parents were Abraham Einstein and Helene Moos, (1808–1868 and 1814–1887, respectively). His parents married in 1839 in Buchau, Germany, and his mother bore eight children, including Hermann, the father to Albert Einstein. Hermann Einstein was sometimes referred to as Hermann Moos. Albert Einstein's father died in 1902, at the age of 55, and when his son, Albert, was only 23 years old, and not yet well-established in life.

Hermann Einstein went to secondary school in Stuttgart, Germany, and at the age of 14, he demonstrated a talent for mathematics and related subjects. However, due to financial restraints, his family could not afford to keep him in school, and he ended up becoming a merchant, partnering with his cousins, Moses and Hermann Levi, in running a bed feathers company.

However, in 1880, when Hermann's brother, Jakob, prompted the family to relocate to Munich, Hermann went with them. Once in Munich, the two brothers established an electrical engineering company, with Hermann served as the merchant and Jakob as the technician. The brothers later relocated to Italy in 1894, re-establishing their engineering company in Pavia.

Mother

Albert Einstein's mother, Pauline Einstein (née Koch), was born on February 8, 1858, in Bad Cannstatt, a German district formerly known as Cannstatt, which is located within Stuttgart in the state of Baden-Württemberg. Pauline's parents were Julius Derzbacher and Jette Bernheimer (1816–1895 and 1825–1886, respectively). Derzbacher, who took up the name Koch in 1842, came from a humble background. Initially from Jebernhausen, he later moved to Cannstatt where he and his brother, Heinreich, established a successful corn trade, building a massive fortune. They also joined the Purveyors to the Royal Court of Württemberg.

Throughout her life, until her death in 1920, her son, Albert, kept in close touch with his mother, Pauline, even as he traveled far from home. Pauline had a sister and two brothers, all older than herself. Her sister's name was Fanny and her brothers were Jacob and Caesar. Although Albert Einstein's mother was both quiet and compassionate, she also was very well-learned. Her talents tended towards the arts, and she played the piano very well. She even influenced her son Albert in learning to play the violin when he was only five years old.

Albert Einstein's mother, Pauline, was 18 years old when she married Hermann on August 8, 1876. Their oldest child, Albert, was born in Ulm; their only other child, a daughter, Maja, was born while they were living in Munic Eisnh. Albert's only sister, Maja, whose name is a version of Maria, was born in 1881 and died in 1951, just four years prior to her brother, Albert's, death.

Sister

Maja was Albert's closest friend as a child, as well as a supportive sister during his brother's scholarly endeavors. She, too, was also brilliant and pursued a successful academic career. Maja's early schooling was in Munich, where she attended elementary school from 1887, to 1894. Later, when their parents relocated to Italy, Maja accompanied them and continued her education at the German International School in Milan. In the meantime, to avoid interrupting his schooling, her brother remained in Munich in the care of relatives. Maja excelled in education, and attended a teachers' workshop in Aarau, from 1899, to 1902. She later specialized in Literature and Romance languages in different institutions in Berlin, Germany, Bern, Switzerland, as well as Paris, France. After her marriage in 1909, Maja continued a close relationship with her brother.

Maja later separated from her husband, Paul Winteler, under difficult circumstances, whom she had married a year after graduating from the University of Bern. During their marriage, the childless couple had become residents of Luzern in 1911, a German-speaking area of Switzerland, and then relocating in 1922 to Colonnata, an ancient village in Italy.

However, in Italy, the ruthless Italian dictator, Benito Mussolini, introduced anti-Semitic laws that were unfavorable to the couple. They sought a way out of the country, with Maja soon joining her brother in America. While excited about being welcomed by Albert and living together in the same residence, Maja found it unfortunate her husband could not join her. Having been denied entry into the U.S. due to his health, the couple never met again.

Maja proved to be a strong, supportive source in both Albert's social and professional life until she passed away in Princeton in 1951 five years after suffering a stroke, from which she had been rendered bedridden, while suffering progressive arteriosclerosis.

Childhood

While many failed to notice Einstein's talents until he was older, his curiosity manifested early. However, at an early age, he was considered to rather pitiable, especially because his speech skills did not develop until he was two years old.

His sister, Maja, later explained that there were people who feared her brother would never be able to learn because of the challenge he faced with language. Some of his early teachers thought him to be handicapped because, even at the age of nine, he could not speak fluently, with the ease and grace of other children his age.

Einstein's family was also not sure whether he was normal or not, either. Their first fears struck them immediately after Albert was born because his head appeared to be so extraordinarily large. While his parents saw this as an abnormality, the physician who attended the birth was not perturbed. However, the baby's head soon shrunk to a normal size and acquired the usual shape. This did not prevent his grandmother, however, the first time she saw her grandchild, from exclaiming that the baby had too much fat. Even with the initial fears gone, Einstein's parents worried further when he reached the age when a child should be uttering words and forming sentences, but their boy child could not speak. They even consulted a doctor.

It is only in retrospect that those acquainted with Albert Einstein say that he was truly extraordinary. While his parents bore their anxiety until their child was four years old, soon something both extraordinary and exciting happened. Once, at dinner time, the apparently dumb child dropped a complete sentence, complaining that the soup was a little too hot. Surprisingly, when he was questioned as to why he had never spoken before, Einstein's response was that it had not been necessary because all was well.

Young Einstein henceforth engaged in conversation with other people; however, he was still not sure of his speech until he was nine years old. Until that age, he would murmur under his breath in preparation for what he wanted to say, and then would only speak when he felt he had it right. Because of this behavior, the housemaid nicknamed him the dopey one, which she termed in German, der Depperte.

Scientific Curiosity

At the age of four, Einstein's father, Hermann, handed him a magnetic compass. The observant Albert noticed that the compass needle was moving without anyone prompting it, and this movement triggered a serious thought process in young Einstein's mind: the needle, which seemed to hold at the North cardinal point, was enclosed in a case, thus protecting it from wind and any other prospective source of pressure. Thereafter, Einstein became extremely interested in mathematics and the workings of science, eventually going on to beat many academic, political, and social odds to become a legend in the world of science. Named the Person of the Century by Time Magazine in Dec 31, 1999, Einstein eventually proved his early childhood critics wrong.

Chapter 2: Early Schooling

Beginning his formal education when he was six years old, the ability to communicate was still a challenge for Einstein. Not surprisingly, he did not make friends. The first school Einstein attended was Petersschule on Blumenstrasse, a Catholic school in the city of Munich. This fact that his first school was Catholic was not especially surprising given that his parents were not strong adherents to the Jewish faith. However, they were particularly keen on sending their child to a school with high academic standards.

Einstein was not social in school, tended to remain quiet, and kept to himself. He detested strict rules that called for absolute obedience. A school routine that was reminiscent of military drills made young Einstein very uncomfortable, and he longed for the play sessions he had with his sister at home. At home, they would play together in creative ways, mostly building card houses.

When Einstein was 10 years old, after he had finally become fluent in speech, his parents enrolled him at Luitpold Gymnasium, a reputable institution. However, the school did not care much for math and science, and instead placed more emphasis on Latin and Greek. A young Einstein was disillusioned. Because he was unable to satisfy the curiosity he had developed in science at this school, he was not happy. Fortunately, Einstein's family understood his concerns and wanted to make his life more fulfilling. For this reason, his uncle Jakob gave Einstein an algebra book. He also sent him mathematical puzzles to solve. This kept the boy's science and math-oriented mind stimulated and engaged. In addition, a family friend, Max Talmud, who was studying medicine, also lent Albert books on science and philosophy. Life for the aspiring scientist thus became more fulfilling as he quickly read the books, absorbing everything he read.

Religion

When Einstein was 11 years old, he became interested in religion. He read the Bible and observed the Jewish kosher dietary laws. Serious in his pursuit of religious knowledge, he began preparing for his Bar Mitzvah. However, soon his scientific knowledge began to conflict with the religious teachings. By the time his peers were preparing to celebrate Bar Mitzvah, at the age of 13, he became resentful of organized religion and its dogma.

While Einstein had at first seemed to have been satisfied with his respectable school, when his father sold his business to relocate to Italy in 1893, taking the rest of the family with him, Einstein did not like being left behind in Germany. Six months later, he feigned an illness by colluding with a doctor he knew. After many pleas from Einstein, the doctor agreed to write him a formal note, stating that he had diagnosed Einstein with neurasthenic exhaustion, or nervous exhaustion.

This made it easy for Einstein to officially leave school, as well as to leave the country before he had completed his education. He was headed to Pavia, Italy, where his parents had settled. It had been only six months since his parents had left for Italy, during which Einstein had resided in a boarding house, where he had become more miserable with each passing day.

The absence of his family was likely not the only reason for Einstein's unhappiness. He also wanted to abandon school and leave Germany early. Many believe Einstein wanted to leave Germany before he turned 17, so that he could avoid being conscripted into the military. According to German laws at the time, any teenager who left Germany before he was seventeen would be exempt from compulsory military service.

Education

Contrary to popular myths about Einstein's education and his attitude towards it, he actually liked it. Some have misconstrued his unhappiness in some educational institutions as a dislike for education; however, this was instead just Einstein's dislike for militaristic routine, as opposed to freedom of thought and behavior.

His parents, too, were likely shocked when, as soon as he arrived in Italy, Einstein expressed some radical views, such as he was no longer interested in adhering to the Jewish faith, and he wanted to relinquish his German citizenship. While this rebellious attitude matched the behavior he later manifested as an adult, including isolating himself in pursuit of his cause, this was in no way any sign of a blind radicalism.

As aforementioned, the discoveries and revelations Einstein had as he pursued science made it so that he saw religious teachings as being in conflict with what he viewed as reality. And when it came to his attitude towards Germany, it was obvious he was upset with anti-Semitic behavior, considering that his family was Jewish.

To allay his parents' fears that his wishing to leave school was not without warrant, he reassured them that he would study seriously and sit for the relevant entrance exam that would allow him to be enrolled at the Federal Swiss Polytechnic in Zurich. The institute offered advanced courses in technical subjects, which shows that Einstein was bent on pursuing the fields of science and mathematics from an early age. At the same time, his asserting his own will to his parents when he was still a teenager shows how independent he was, as well as how strong his convictions were.

However, Einstein's wish to enter his chosen institution of learning may have been overly ambitious at the time, especially when thinking that he could pass such a technical entrance exam without formal guidance. Despite studying on his own during the summer of 1895, Einstein did not pass the entry exam to the Zurich Polytechnic that he sat for in October of that year. However, he was subsequently accepted.

The principal must have admired Einstein's determination and exemplary strength in mathematics because he advised Einstein not to return to Italy, and instead to stay in Aarau and attend a Swiss Secondary

School. Clearly, the course material he had abandoned at the gymnasium in Germany had come back to haunt him.

Some have cited Einstein's failing this entrance examination as supportive of the notion the later world-renowned physicist was not a brilliant student, which is not the case. Beside the fact Einstein had not yet completed his secondary school courses at the time of attempting the exam, he was also underage. The entry age for the college was 18 years old and above; however, Einstein was only 15½ years old at the time. In fact, in order to be permitted to sit for the examination, a family friend, Gustav Maier, had to put in a good word for him, persuading the director of the polytechnic, Albin Herzog, to allow Einstein to sit for the exam.

Aarau, Switzerland

At the age of 16, Einstein stayed with a host family in Aarau while attending school, and in preparation for his anticipated college entry exam. Usually, students preparing to join the institution were already 18 years old. His host was Professor Jost Winteler, who had a large family of seven children and was also a well-known philologist, who taught linguistics and history.

During the time Einstein was dedicated to learning at the school that was 20 miles away from Zurich, he was also maturing socially, so he had a good time in Aarau. He got on very well with Professor Winteler's children, and even entered into a romantic relationship with one of the girls, Marie Winteler. However, the relationship did not mature to anything more serious, and Einstein later got involved with another, Mileva Maric, whom he would later marry.

Not a Social Outcast

Aside from his romantic involvement with Marie Winteler, Einstein also developed close friendships with two of her siblings, Paul and Anna. Paul Winteler eventually ended up marrying Albert Einstein's sister, Maja. Anna Winteler married Einstein's close friend, Michelangelo Besso, a Swiss Italian who was six years older than Albert. Besso studied engineering, which was what Albert's father had wanted his son to pursue, and he also played the violin. In fact, their first encounter, in 1896, had been at a concert.

Einstein's stay at Aarau was memorable. When he left, he was a self-assured, confident young man, as well as communicative. This demeanor was in stark contrast to what it had been when he was in Germany. Einstein was no longer the lonely boy.

Chapter 3: Exciting Journey Before 30

The Einstein whom many had previously thought was incapacitated was soon to turn out to be a genius unlike the world had ever seen. After acquiring fluency of speech and satisfying his curiosity by studying science, the character of young Einstein became distinctive.

It was already evident that Einstein had a mind of his own from an early age. For example, attending the technical institute at Zurich was his personal choice, just as his abandoning the gymnasium in Germany had been his decision. Usually, those are decisions that teenagers his age only make in consultation with their parents, doing so as requests.

The confident Einstein of Aarau only became more self-assured after he graduated from college. No longer worried about his intellect and abilities, his parents were instead eager to see him set even greater goals for himself. He did not disappoint. Einstein pursued his scientific goals relentlessly. (After his fame years later, the secondary school he had attended in Germany was named in his honor, as the Albert Einstein Gymnasium.) In spite of successfully pursuing his scholarly interests, Einstein still faced challenges. With his father's failing health and the family business doing poorly, the young Einstein, in particular, felt the burden when his father died.

Music

Although Einstein's mother had introduced him to the violin at the tender age of five, he did not play the instrument seriously until he was 13 years old. At that time, he began to explore music and to appreciate Mozart's violin sonatas. Thereafter, he would play the violin in string quartets until he was an adult. He once told one of his friends that Mozart's music was so pure and beautiful that he saw it as a real reflection of the universe's inner beauty.

First Serious Scientific Article

While Einstein wrote at least 300 scientific papers over the course of his life, he notably wrote his first scientific paper as a teenager. Although the article was not published until he was 22 years old, he wrote it in 1895 when he was 16 years old, soon after moving to northern Italy with his family.

Despite the common rumors that are often told in stories about prominent people, Einstein did not magically make his discoveries as an adult. And he was not the daft child that some have thought. While he was slow in speech, he was not stupid. As far as academics were concerned, he had his likes and dislikes, just like any other normal child. Einstein's preferences were mathematics and physics, and in these he excelled. In his official report card dated, Sept 30, 1896, Einstein scored the highest grades possible in physics, math and related subjects.

Teaching Diploma in Physics

After attending secondary school in Switzerland, and later qualifying to join Zürich Polytechnic, Einstein acquired a teaching diploma in 1900. Although his schoolwork was exemplary in physics, his grades in math were not impressive, most likely because Einstein did not give the subject serious attention at the time. Later, as an adult, he explained that when young he had not yet appreciated that the fundamental principles of physics were linked to the most complex methods of mathematics.

Socialism

Many are influenced into changing their own world views when associating with others with different ideologies. However, this was not the case with Albert Einstein, who began to embrace socialism at the age of 23. Einstein's interest in socialism began after witnessing his father, Hermann, struggle with a failing business. Herman later fell ill and died in 1902. Albert did not have a job at the time, and the family owed Albert's uncle a large amount of money, debt the older Einstein had left behind. At only 23, Albert Einstein found that he was expected to provide for his jobless mother and younger sister.

The challenge of providing for his family got Einstein thinking about how much easier it would be if they had been living in a socialist country. He attributed the financial mess the family was in to capitalism, and this made him in favor of socialism. Later in life, he envisioned a world where all nations of operated under a universal government.

First Born

Not only did Einstein have his first born child at the age of 23, the child was also born out of wedlock. It was 1902, the same year Einstein lost his father, a difficult time for him. The child's mother was Mileva Marić, was the girl he had met while attending college in Zurich. Mileva Marić, Einstein's college friend in Zurich, did not graduate. However, the two young lovers married in 1903. It is not known what happened to the child; however, conspiracy theories abound, including that the child was given up for adoption. More recently, it is believed the child died from scarlet fever. Then, at the age of 25, Einstein and his wife, Marić, bore their second child, a son, whom they named Hans Albert Einstein.

Failed to Gain a Job in Academia

In the academic world, one must have higher degrees; these Einstein did not yet have, other than a physics diploma from Zurich Polytechnic. For this reason, he could not yet gain a position in any institution of higher learning, so he had to look elsewhere for an income.

A Clerk

In spite of his brilliance, Einstein took up a clerical job in Germany, where he worked in the Patent Office at the federal office. After working for two years in the

Bern office, Einstein had rapidly managed to publish four scientific articles, one after the other. During this period he introduced his Special Theory of Relativity, for which he later became famous. These four articles appeared in the prestigious Annals of Physics.

University Of Bern

Even though Einstein knew he was brilliant, he was not an arrogant man. In 1908 he accepted work as an apprentice at the University of Bern, on a temporary basis. However, he was unable to continue after two semesters because of a lack of students. By the time he decided to cancel his classes, the attendance had diminished to only a single student.

Employment in Academia

By now, Einstein's star was beginning to shine. In 1909, he received an offer from the University of Zurich, asking him to take up a lecturer's position on a permanent basis. However honored he may have been, he nevertheless turned down the offer because of the small salary that was offered. In comparison, his pay at the federal office was higher.

Soon thereafter, the University of Zurich raised the pay for the job they had offered, and so Einstein accepted it. He subsequently humorously described to a colleague in a letter the good news that he, too, had officially joined the "guild of whores."

Chapter 4: Influences

The negative attitude of Einstein's family, teachers, and others that Einstein experienced as a child due to his speech challenges was not unusual. However, what was extraordinary was the fact that Einstein never allowed others' attitudes, fears, and labels to determine his life's path. They never made him question his own abilities or thwarted him from his goals.

Instead, Einstein ignored the naysayers, carefully avoided unwelcome company, and invested his time alone intellectually evaluating things he had observed, trying to understand how those things had happened, and to find their meanings. His curiosity was evident from the time he had received a magnetic compass from his father. His mind worked to know what invisible forces were behind the moving of the solitary needle.

Nevertheless, Einstein's life may have turned out differently if certain events had not taken place the way they did and when they did. He would have taken longer to make his mark in the world of science. While some of the events of Einstein's life may appear to be insignificant, the reality is that many others tend to be thwarted in their pursuits by the circumstances that affect them.

Einstein's family was small and close, and when Einstein's father, Hermann, moved to Italy for business, leaving his son behind, it greatly affected the young Einstein. While it has already been noted how pivotal his father's act of giving him a compass was in his interest and future pursuits of physics, it has also been noted how useful the literature provided by his uncle was at an early age. Needless to say, then, the two men were very much a part of Albert's support system, and being abruptly disengaged from both of them must have affected him.

In fact, there exist reports in which Pauline Einstein, Albert's mother, states that leaving her son behind to accompany her husband and brother-in-law to Pavia, Italy, took a toll on her. Normally, when a familial relationship has been close, the agony of disengagement is experienced by both parties. In young Einstein's case, it appears that he suffered inwardly, not being very expressive at that stage in life.

Two years after his family's move to Italy, the business that Einstein's father co-owned with Einstein's uncle Jakob failed; they abandoned it in 1896. Einstein, however, was still close enough to witness his father's business struggles because he had only remained in Munich for six months after the family's relocation to Italy. Understanding the questioning mind Albert had, one can safely assume he had questioned the reason for his family's financial troubles, and whether something could have been done differently to change his family's difficult experiences.

While Einstein may not have come up with any extraordinary business solutions, his attitude towards a free market and capitalism definitely changed. And while apparently no direct complaints from him have been recorded, Einstein could not see any good reason why a family such as his should have suffered so much financially, especially when his parents were hard working, enterprising, and determined.

Einstein watched his father be proactive in his endeavors, leaving the first business partnership he had with his brother, and relocating to Milan to begin his own electrical engineering company. While the business in Milan did better than the earlier one in Pavia had done, its performance was still not great. To make matters worse, even before Albert could do much of anything with his diploma in physics that he had obtained in Zurich, he watched his father, the family breadwinner, fail in health and die. It was devastating for Einstein when his father died of heart failure.

From this undoubtedly agonizing experience, it is no wonder that Einstein chose to turn his back to capitalism and to embrace socialism. He refused to back a system that enabled hard working people to suffer, just as he refused to embrace Mussolini's unwarranted discrimination on the basis of race.

Chapter 5: Science Should Not Be Overrated

While the greatest physicist, Einstein was no lab rat. He preferred instead to do his thinking in a free environment, one least affected by constraining rules, formulae, and apparatus. He was most comfortable thinking critically, in what can generally be termed a natural human habitat.

And while that sounds as if someone who would fit squarely in the field of arts, this, of course, was not the case with Einstein. His work was not based on fantasy, but on imagination that was based on observation and facts; his critical thinking was more factual, as well as more accurately calculated and evaluated. His work in theoretical physics has actually been recognized by experts in experimental physics, further supporting a reason why the two categories of physics should coexist.

Unlike artists, Einstein notably theorized matter in a way that brought his visualization very close, if not exactly, in line with practical results. In fact, scientists agree on the importance of both theoretical and experimental physics. When one is good at theoretical physics, it means one can provide a basis on which to forecast events, a valuable feat that can help to preempt danger or to prepare for eventualities.

It is also a fact that some of the most notorious eventualities cannot be experimented on or tested in advance – at least not in a realistic way. Therefore, this places the burden on theoretical scientists to conjure up realistic situations and outcomes, and with the help of experimental scientists, the best means to handle such situations.

For instance, how can someone can stand at an epicenter knowing that an earthquake is imminent, even in the pursuit of scientific study? Of course, there the hurricane chasers, who do it for the thrill, even with full knowledge the storm could turn into a tornado traveling at the speed of a car. In any case, such thrill seekers cannot negate the need for scientific research because predictions, whether scientific or not, are usually meant to work within the realms of possibility.

Therefore, it is left to theoretical scientists, such as Einstein, to theorize in advance, and to make observations and deductions to serve scientific and other purposes. For instance, The American Journal reported that a long-held scientific theory, Igneous Rock Theory, has been called into question. Oddly enough, those who questioned the validity of this theory are everyday folk–journalists and residents who have watched a series of earthquakes happen over time. Scientific revelations are not only the prerogative of learned scientists.

Instead of the prevailing theory, some everyday people, including a journalist and an ordinary resident of an earthquake prone area in Britain, have found that the long-held belief that earthquakes result from the eruption of molten rock is wanting. They have observed instead that there are some places that have been hit with earthquakes, even when no volcanic eruption had taken place in the same period. In short, according to the critics, the assertion that earthquakes and volcanic eruptions go hand in hand may be misleading.

Not the Alpha And Omega

Einstein's attitude towards academia, including how unnecessarily exclusive the academic community can be, is liberating to brilliant minds outside of academia, who would otherwise not contribute to society just because they could not get their names into the register of academicians. Many are still embarrassed that there were students who missed the opportunity to learn from the brilliant Albert Einstein, simply because he could not secure a job in institutions of higher learning with only his diploma in physics. However, he nevertheless went on to distinguish himself from everyone else, including those who had Ph.D.'s. He did eventually earn a doctoral degree.

What has thus far been presented in this chapter is a preamble to the discussion that follows on one of Albert Einstein's published papers, Why Socialism. Since Einstein had unabashedly acknowledged embracing socialism, he later went on to explain in the article why he thought it was superior to capitalism. However, before doing so, he gave a justification for a scientist such as himself to give his views on social and economic issues. As far as he was concerned, it was not necessary to be an expert in the field of economics, or other, social, fields to be in a position to comment on related issues.

Chapter 6: Not Responsible For the Atomic Bomb

Among the mysteries surrounding Albeit Einstein is whether or not he was the scientific force behind the atomic bombs the U. S. made that wreaked havoc and destruction in Japan. To find out the truth, it is important to look at what was going on in the world in that era, how much Einstein knew about the art of bomb-making, and how involved he was with the U.S. government.

When WWII was raging and U.S. soldiers were dying in huge numbers, Einstein found himself at odds with some of the countries the U.S. was fighting against, such as Germany and Italy, in the main because of their repressive and discriminatory regimes. However, in spite of his bad feelings towards these regimes, Einstein had no control over the U.S. bomb-making project, let alone how the bombs were used.

If you ever hear the word "gadget" in reference to WWII, it means the first atomic bomb the U.S. made in preparation to counter aggression from Nazi Germany. Obviously, such a dangerous weapon required highly scientific skills, and considering Einstein became famous for his physics genius long before WWII, one might well expect that he was on the panel that developed and executed the project.

However, not everyone wants the answer to that question because of Einstein's standing in the field of physics. They often speak about it as if Einstein being a part of the atomic bomb project was a foregone conclusion. However, the reality is that Einstein was not actually on the panel that organized the making of America's first atomic bomb, nor any of the others. Did he know about the bomb making plans? Yes. Did he provide input? Yes. Therefore, the question is how much of a role did he play?

In 1938, three years into WWII, scientists based in Berlin, Germany, managed to split a uranium atom, while conducting scientific experiments. They knew right away the potential such a capability held, since splitting atoms could produce power of massive proportions. Needless to say, any government could utilize this ability to wield this power to its advantage. In times of war, this could, of course, meant using such a capacity to the detriment of rival countries.

Interestingly, following this unexpected discovery, Germany did not rush to make an atomic bomb because further processes needed to be put in place first, such as to ensure the stability of the bomb once manufactured, and that it was safe for the handlers during delivery, and so on. However, someone leaked the news to fellow scientists, and Einstein got the news, as did another scientist, Enrico Fermi.

Einstein hated the Nazi regime from which he had escaped, and Fermi had come to the U.S. to seek refuge from fascism in Italy. Combining the forces of Einstein and Fermi against Germany and its allies, including Italy was, therefore, the most natural thing. Both felt they owed their host country, the U.S., loyalty. Fermi was the first emissary to travel to Washington, which he did in March 1938. His mission was to pass the message to top government officials that German scientists had stumbled upon discoveries that could enable Germany to manufacture a bomb and to use it on the U.S. While Fermi may have expected quick action from the U.S. government, that did not happen.

Germany

When Einstein was convinced there was a possibility of German scientists actually making a bomb, he decided to warn President Roosevelt directly, instead of going through junior staff and hitting a dead end as his colleague, Fermi, had. Therefore, in 1939, he wrote a letter to the president in which he told him what he knew about Germany's potential to make a bomb. It is that letter for which Albert Einstein is considered to have influenced the U.S. in its decision to manufacture an atomic bomb. Nevertheless, there seemed to be no hurry in manufacturing the deadly weapon. And the president did not appoint Einstein to a bomb manufacturing panel, or have him join an already-formed panel. As aforementioned, Einstein never liked working under stringent protocols anyway.

U.S. Army Intelligence

Although President Roosevelt appreciated the warning from Einstein, the president did not seem overly excited about the prospects of the U.S. making an atomic bomb. Nevertheless, it must have been a surprise when

Einstein was denied security clearance by the U.S. Army, which would have enabled him access to the Manhattan project. Einstein certainly would have liked to witness the workings of such a massive project, not necessarily for political reasons, or for prestige, but for scholarly and scientific reasons. After all, the project fell squarely within his field of specialization.

U.S. Intelligence may not have given reasons for denying the topmost scientist a security clearance; however, it is easy to make fairly accurate deductions. The people concerned with the vetting believed they could not trust Einstein whose left-leaning political views were a matter of public knowledge. And since apparently no one cared to find out to exactly how far his socialist ideals went, Einstein had to be content with waiting like the average American to see what would come after this scientific breakthrough.

Fermi

When the decision was made that the U.S. was going to try to make an atomic bomb, a few top institutions and scientists were involved. Columbia University, University of California, and the University of Chicago were the three institutions involved from the beginning. The services of Einstein's colleague and friend, Enrico Fermi, were also sought, even while Einstein was left out.

The Manhattan project had to be undertaken in a cautious manner, as the U.S. had to do its own research and tests, too. In 1940, there were indications from experiments done in the U.S. that making an atomic was feasible. More tests confirmed definitively that the U.S. could actually make the atomic bomb. During these tests, scientists further discovered that plutonium could be of use in the bomb-making process.

Thus the results of the disclosure by Einstein about the discoveries of German scientists began to take shape in December 1941. This was when the U.S. government launched the bomb-making project under the code name, the Manhattan Project, for which a select group of scientists worked in collaboration with the U.S. military. The very first breakthrough came under the leadership of Fermi, when, in December 1942, a nuclear chain reaction was produced at Stagg Field, a football field at the University of Chicago.

While Einstein clearly did not take part in the actual making of the atomic bomb, the project had his blessings. He was also not involved in May 1945 when the team of scientists tested the bomb-monitoring instruments in the town of Los Alamos, New Mexico, nor was he there on July 16 when they detonated the bomb in New Mexico.

Japan

U.S. scientists, the army, the government and the public were excited by the historic scientific milestone the U.S. had achieved. However, Germany, whose scientific discovery had triggered the Manhattan Project, had surrendered on May 7, 1945.

However, since Japan was still a problem, the U.S. decided to use the bomb to weaken Japan's strength in ongoing war. On Aug 6, 1945, the U.S. dropped an atomic bomb on the city of Hiroshima. The U.S. bomb-making team had codenamed the bomb, Little Boy. And while Japan was still reeling from the devastation on Hiroshima, the U.S. unleashed even more destruction on Nagasaki on Aug 9, 1945 with another atomic bomb.

When Einstein heard that the U.S. had hit Hiroshima with an atomic bomb, he painfully exclaimed, "Woe is me." He never wished for Japan to be bombed. In fact, he expressed sadness about the way the U.S. had used its bombs. He told Newsweek he would not have mentioned anything to President Roosevelt if he ever had a reason to believe Germany would not succeed in making an atomic bomb. Nevertheless, without any prior planning or initiative, Einstein did, in fact, have a hand in ushering in the Nuclear era.

Prejudice

If there was one thing that made Einstein's stomach turn it was prejudice. He greatly disliked life under Nazi Germany, and he felt for his sister who had to experience life under Mussolini of Italy. It is no wonder Einstein did not hesitate to invite his sister to his home in the U.S. when she found life intolerable in Italy.

After settling in the U.S., and as Einstein interacted with people both within and outside of academia, he realized the country had its prejudices, too. He witnessed the discrimination against African Americans firsthand, which reminded him of the discrimination Jews were facing in Germany. As a true scientist, however, he was a practical man, and he did not just sit and watch as a minority was discriminated against, just because he was not the victim at the time. On the contrary, Einstein spoke out. He found the time to see what was happening in the world outside of science and academics in general and did what he could do to influence things in a positive manner.

Fame

A number of celebrities do put their fame to good use. However, not as much is heard about academicians once they are thrust into the limelight. This was not the case with Einstein, a man who knew what it was like to be shunned for aspects of life beyond his control. After all, when, as a child, many had looked down upon him, speaking about him as if he was retarded, only because his speech system was underdeveloped. However, of course, later Einstein became famous internationally when he won the Nobel Prize.

Soon after the First World War (WWI), in 1919, Arthur Eddington, a British astronomer, with his team of experts, confirmed Albert Einstein's Theory of Relativity. Einstein's name immediately spread across the world as the news of his theory broke. Any newspapers of substance ran a headline for his achievement, such as The New York Times, The Times of London, and others.

Although Einstein was pleased with affirmation of his work, he also considered what his fame could do to improve humanity. For this reason, he did not shy away from meeting other famous people, such as Charlie Chaplin, the popular English comedian, or even the Queen of Belgium. He understood that such famous people would help him get his message across. He revived his old feelings about Germany, the country he had chosen to disown when he renounced his citizenship soon after leaving secondary school at sixteen years of age, and began to speak openly about the need to end the militarism that was the hallmark of German rule. He even advocated that Germany cease to subject its citizens to mandatory military service, which he had escaped from when he abandoned his school in Germany to follow his parents to Italy.

Einstein thus began to speak openly for the rights of Jews, underlining the fact he was primarily a Jew, even if he was born in Germany. By virtue of his fame, he was able to reach out to well-wishers and to raise funds to support the Hebrew University in Jerusalem. Einstein did not just merely speak out about people's rights in interviews with journalists; he also often wrote about what his stance was without fear whenever he had the opportunity to do so.

As Einstein got to know people in the U.S., he also found the opportunity to support his fellow Jews, who, at the time, had no formal state of their own. Kurt Blumenfeld, a Zionist movement leader, had already met Einstein and had asked for his support in advocating for the establishment of a Jewish state in

Palestine. However, when Einstein became famous with his scientific theory, Blumenfeld returned to him with a message from the World Zionist Organization's president, Chaim Weizmann. Weizmann wanted Einstein to pay him a visit.

Weizmann was an expert in biochemistry who had left Russia to live in England, and who had helped his host country immensely during WWI. He had assisted England by showing the British scientists more efficient ways of making explosives, as they engaged in war during the term of the Prime Minister, Arthur Balfour. In his response to Weizmann, Einstein said he realized he now had an obligation to do what he could to help his fellow Jews. He even declared he was doing everything in his power to help the Jewish people who had been treated badly wherever they were.

Blumenfeld was also pleasantly surprised by Einstein's readiness to engage in matters of public interest beyond physics. Two years before he had known him as a person who had shied from the limelight, but now, in 1921, Einstein's enthusiasm amazed him. It was clear that his stint in Berlin had made him conscious of his race as a Jewish person, and thus he was prepared to use his fame to help to restore the dignity of his people.

Germany

While Einstein's scientific and theoretical breakthroughs brought him instant fame, the way he utilized that fame, while endearing him to many, particularly the oppressed, antagonized him to others.

People who bore anti-Semitic attitudes, especially those in Germany, were irritated by Einstein's outspokenness on matters of human rights.

One such person who had a lot of disdain for Einstein was Philipp Lenard, himself a Nobel Prize winner. The hatred he demonstrated against Einstein's support for the Jews and other disadvantaged groups is not surprising, as Lenard identified with the Nazis, eventually becoming one of them. In 1921, when Einstein was nominated for the Nobel Prize in Physics, Lenard did all he could behind the scenes to prevent Einstein from being awarded the prize. He, and others with similar attitudes towards Einstein, put pressure on the Nobel Committee to the extent it withheld the award that year, not giving it to anyone.

Nevertheless, the anti-Einstein group did not get away with this undue influence, and the following year, the Nobel Prize committee belatedly awarded the physics prize to Einstein. He received it at the same time as Niels Henrik David Bohr, a Danish physicist, who also won the 1922 Nobel Prize in Physics.

Limelight

When Albert Einstein made headlines across the globe, and he began to capitalize on his fame for the good of others, his friends knew he would soon be stepping on some toes. One of his colleagues, and a dear friend who had advised him to keep out of the public limelight, was Paul Ehrenfest. He had done so after reading an article Einstein had written that he knew would rub Philipp

Lenard the wrong way, and he had even asked his friend to apologize to Lenard, but Einstein declined. Ehrenfest had termed the public a "voracious beast," that Einstein needed to stop feeding.

Ignoring Ehrenfest meant Einstein had deep convictions about what he was doing. Ehrenfest was a dear friend whom he respected. Even in his work on the Influence of Gravitation on the Propagation of Light, where Einstein draws attention to the way rays are diffracted near the sun, he mentions the time he and Ehrenfest had spent together in Prague, when Ehrenfest was on a visit from St. Petersburg. He highlighted the time they shared together socially and while playing music, as well as physicists exchanging ideas, as the most beautiful part of his stay in Prague.

During the same period, Einstein received even stronger pressure from other friends, including Max and Hedwig Born. They urged Einstein to avoid courting the limelight, advising him to heed his friends and colleagues, who knew better what it meant to be in the public eye. Max even wrote to him to emphasize his point. Many of his scientist colleagues were of a similar opinion as well.

Anti-Semitism

Einstein's friends were right about his courting trouble. Soon, scientists with anti-Semitic attitudes were up in arms. They began with disguising their hatred for Einstein by criticizing his scholarly work and scientific findings. Their fight against Einstein went on for years, culminating with the release by a German publisher of the book, One Hundred Authors Against Einstein.

Although the book that is comprised of essays by different authors sought to invalidate Einstein's theory of relativity, some essays were blatantly anti-Semitic. His Jewish identity was now being used by his detractors to attack his work in science. As unethical as this may seem, Einstein himself was using his Jewish background to draw attention to the plight of disadvantaged communities, not only Jews, but also African Americans.

Once Einstein was speaking with Peter Bucky, whose family and that of Einstein's were very close, explaining to him that it was easy to empathize with marginalized groups of people, because as a Jew, he had experienced similar marginalization and prejudices. In short, Einstein did not hesitate to invoke his status as a Jewish person to get his point across.

Admirers

In spite of the hate of anti-Semitic scientists, Einstein was still making a positive impact on particular communities, not only for the Jews, but also for African Americans and others.

Einstein is, in fact, well-remembered for his unequivocal criticism against the handlers of the Scottsboro Boys trial, which took place in Alabama in 1931, and which later became symbolic of a blatant miscarriage of justice that had been driven by racial prejudice. In 1931, Einstein joined a committee led by Theodore Dreiser, the writer, to protest the prejudicial handling of the case.

The Scottsboro Boys case involved nine boys of African American descent, who were put on trial in the city of Scottsboro, in the state of Alabama. They had been accused of raping two white women, when it was actually a case of retaliation by white boys, who had initiated a racially-driven brawl between themselves and the black boys, while on a train heading to Memphis, Tennessee. The white boys' egos were injured as they left the train midway through journey, and their way of retaliation was to report to the police that they had been attacked on the train by a group of black boys.

The accusation escalated from a case of assault, to rape, when the police got the train intercepted at Paint Rock, another Alabama town. As the police searched the train, two white women, who had remained on the train, accused the group of black boys of having raped them. The courts declared the boys guilty and sentenced them to death, with the exception of one boy who was only 12 years old at the time. It did not matter to the court that medical evidence had shown the boys had, in fact, not raped the women.

Du Bois and the NAACP

Einstein was not yet done condemning oppressors, and he was also not done encouraging minorities to resist oppression. He thus gladly accepted an invitation the same year from W.E.B. Du Bois, a prominent African

American, to write a piece for his magazine, The Crisis. Du Bois, a sociologist, was a respected person within the African American community, and a co-founder of NAACP.

Building on the opportunity provided by Du Bois, Einstein applauded the people who were agitating for civil rights, while urging African Americans to stand tall, and to resist the efforts made to put them down. He encouraged them to maintain their sense of self-worth, regardless of the discrimination they encountered. He advised them to forge closer unions among themselves, and to educate their people regarding their rights and related matters, and that finally their souls would be emancipated.

It is worth noting that, while Einstein found issues he did not like in America, he still appreciated the freedom of expression he enjoyed. It was unlikely he could have made such criticisms against Germany and its institutions from within that country, without risking his life. In fact, when Einstein received a permanent job offer from the Institute of Advanced Study in New Jersey in 1933, he was excited about leaving Europe to settle in the U.S.

Anti-Communism

Einstein had turned into a hero for oppressed minorities; however, at the same time he created enemies from the people whom he would otherwise not have had problems with. In the fight for justice for the Scottsboro Boys, Einstein had joined hands with different groups on the same mission. Not only did those groups include the National Association for the Advancement of Colored People (NAACP), but they also included the Communist Party that had been formed in 1919, after splitting from the Socialist Party of America. Some people saw Einstein's liaison with the Communist Party as betrayal for his country of residence. Thus, solely on those grounds, anti-communists also joined in the chorus of Einstein's enemies.

Even distinguished scholars criticized Einstein's behavior. One such critic was Robert Millikan, who had won the Nobel Prize for Physics two years after Einstein. His stance was that Einstein should not have joined left-wing groups and their complaints and protests against the handling of the Scottsboro Boys trial.

This must have surprised Einstein, coming from a man as informed as Millikan, considering Einstein's interest in the case was judicial and social justice, as opposed to forging political alliances. More surprising still for Einstein, however, was Millikan's subsequent daring to try to recruit Einstein to join Caltech, an institution of higher learning associated with Millikan. Criticism came from other sectors, too, including business. Ford reproduced the outrageous essays that had been published earlier in Germany, in a bid to discredit Einstein and to demean him.

Chapter 7: Passion

The question of whether or not Einstein was brilliant has already been answered. Whether he was naturally talented is also not in doubt. With this talent, he excelled to the extent of receiving a Nobel Prize. In doing so, he actually redefined the way people perceive space, gravity, and time with his famous Theory of Relativity.

Impressive as that is, there are many who would have expected him to delve wider into the arena of science, considering he was still energetic and vivacious when he received the Nobel Prize in Physics. Nevertheless, he spent a good part of the latter years of his life advancing the cause of the marginalized. In fact, during the last twenty years of his eventful life, he promoted causes outside the scope of science, for which he was passionate about. This passion seemed to have catapulted him from a public-shy individual, to an attention-seeking activist.

Needless to say, Einstein was fed up with Germany by the time he left his job in Berlin, not because of anything to do with his academic or scientific pursuits, but because of the insensitivity of the regime in matters that affected the dignity of some people, and the culture of discrimination among many people of German descent, who saw themselves as nationalists.

His move to the U.S., therefore, can be termed a breath of fresh air. In spite of the idea he had of a free America, he was disappointed to realize some groups were seriously marginalized, as well as to witness this firsthand. At Princeton University, where he began to work on arrival from Germany, the institution, in fact, did not enroll African American students simply because they were black. And elsewhere in the U.S., racial segregation was prevalent.

For example, anyone whose complexion was black could not enjoy entertainment in theaters with whites. They also could not attend the same schools. The treatment blacks received from whites resonated with the harassment Einstein had received from the Nazis in Germany for being Jewish. It was, therefore, natural for Einstein to stand up for the blacks, and to speak out against racial discrimination.

In the book, Einstein on Race and Racism, published in 2006 by a university press, the authors point out that Einstein understood that segregation in the U.S., and mistreatment of the Jews by Germans, were two similar evils. As such, for Einstein, seeing whites discriminate against blacks greatly disturbed him.

Since racial discrimination in the U.S. was basically a part of the culture, Einstein witnessed it on a daily basis, while doing what he could to speak out against it, and to show his discontent. However, the mainstream media, which was dominated by a pro-white stance, blacked out Einstein's protest speeches. They even ignored his documented protests and appeals because they called for civil rights.

Civil Rights

The public support Einstein declared for the victims of the infamous Scottsboro Boys trial led the list of actions that he took to show that he was greatly opposed to discrimination. Another incident occurred when the Metropolitan Opera star, Marian Anderson, was denied a room at the Nassau Inn, in Princeton, just because she was not white. Einstein did not hesitate to host her instead, not just to save Anderson a lot of inconvenience, but also to make his stand known that he was opposed to acts of racial discrimination. From that time in 1937, Einstein's friendship with the contralto opera personality took root, and they remained friends until Einstein's death. In fact, Einstein served as her host each time she was in Princeton.

Einstein gave a speech against racism at the University of Lincoln in Pennsylvania, in 1946. Historically known as a university for African Americans, it was, in fact, the university where the famous American poet, novelist, and social activist, Langston Hughes, and Thurgood Marshall, a prominent American lawyer, studied. The university gave Einstein an honorary degree which he respectfully accepted. Since Einstein was known to turn down invitations from universities, everyone was excited about Einstein's visit when they learned he was to honor their invitation. Gladly, he did not disappoint. He memorably spoke of racism as the white people's disease. And, of course, the academic community got to hear about the subject of relativity from the guru himself, as Einstein was also happy to give a lecture on it.

Einstein not only fought for the rights of the oppressed, he also did so boldly. In 1946, after Paul Robeson, an actor of African-American decent who was blacklisted for his role in as a civil rights advocate, Einstein joined hands with Robeson to advance their anti-lynching cause. Not surprisingly, due to the blacklisting, Robeson's career took a nosedive. However, Einstein was on hand to provide support. He invited Robeson to his home at Princeton in 1952 when things became very tough due to the damage done to his career, and he did not care what the whites would say. Actually, he hoped hosting Robeson would make a statement that declared the backed Robeson's position on civil rights, and also that he was disgusted by the public castigation of Robeson.

When it came to support for African Americans in the U.S., Einstein worked with the NAACP for decades. He spoke out publicly about the unfair treatment African Americas experienced by white Americans. Einstein was still supporting W.E.B. Du Bois in 1951, when, at an advanced age of 83, Du Bois was indicted by the federal government and labeled a foreign agent. The judge found himself in a precarious position when Einstein offered to appear in court in person to serve as Du Bois' character witness. Aware of the international publicity the trial was bound to elicit, the judge dropped the case.

Einstein was always bold when it came to expressing his beliefs, and his likes and dislikes. In 1946, he published an essay in the January issue of Pageant Magazine, "The Negro Question," which is often cited. In the essay, Einstein wrote that America's worst disease was racism, and that what America took to be equality and human dignity was, unfortunately, only limited to white men.

Einstein wrote further that since he had acquired American citizenship, he could not afford to be complacent when he saw racial discrimination. He stated that if he did not speak out against such prejudice, he would consider himself as guilty as those who perpetrated the evil of discrimination. Einstein also noted that he had also experienced discrimination as a Jew living among the whites in the U.S., but that what he experienced was not compared to what African Americans experienced.

Chapter 8: Student Life

Einstein had left Luitpold Gymnasium with a certificate indicating that he had qualified in mathematics, and thus he would be able to attend university. However, upon joining his father in Pavia, Hermann was not especially excited about the direction Albert seemed to have been taking. He advised Albert instead to pursue a career in engineering, which, to the elder Einstein, was a practical field that would help his son make a living.

When Albert remained adamant about mathematics and physics, his father then used his connections to get Albert a waiver that would allow the institution to ignore his young age. With the age issue aside, during the month of September 1895, Einstein sat for the entrance exam, a prerequisite to join the Zurich Polytechnic.

Unfortunately, however, the languages and history sections did not go well for the young Einstein, so he failed the entrance exam. This is why Einstein eventually landed at the Aargau Canton School, in Aarau, where he found dedicated teachers and a liberal environment that he enjoyed.

The Wintelers

Einstein was not only brilliant, but also charming. During his stay in Aarau, he was considered to be a handsome young man, with brown eyes and curly hair. His height was average. As a young man, he was very different from what people who had only seen him as a child would have expected. He was now outgoing, no longer reserved. Soon, he also began to develop romantic feelings towards the Wintelers' youngest daughter, Marie.

The young Einstein even told his mother about the romance; and in a letter to Marie, Einstein disclosed that his mother had approved of the relationship. Einstein called his first girlfriend his "Little Sunshine."

At the home of Professor Winteler, who hosted Albert, it was all joy and debate. Einstein loved it there. With a large family of seven children, parents, and frequent visitors, spirited discussions were the order of the day. The family would also often hold social gatherings, and the usual discussions would be enriched with intellectual brainstorming. As Einstein still enjoyed music, he would play the violin, which everyone appreciated immensely.

All seemed to have been going well for Albert, until he learned of how badly his father's business back in Pavia was doing. During the end of the spring in 1896, Albert learned that his father had gone bankrupt. He had exhausted every penny his wife had as well and still owed other members of the family. As such, he could not continue to finance young Einstein's education. This would turn out to be a very frustrating time for the young Einstein: His education at Aargau Canton School was in jeopardy.

Fortunately, Einstein's affluent maternal aunt, Julie Koch, who lived in Genoa, Italy, volunteered to give her nephew 100 Francs every month, until he completed his studies at the school.

After Einstein had passed the secondary school exam, or what is otherwise known as the Matura examination, he relocated to Zurich to join the Polytechnic he had wanted to join from the very beginning. However, there was still one small matter. Einstein was now 17, the required age of military service in his home country of Germany. Obviously, he did not want to enlist.

German Citizenship

Just as his father had used his connections to guide Albert to the Zurich Polytechnic, he also helped Albert evade military service in Germany by sorting out the issue of his citizenship. Since the time young Einstein had arrived in Pavia, he had expressed his wish to drop his German citizenship, and now his father did not hesitate to request that the German government terminate his son's citizenship. In January of 1896, Hermann Einstein's request was granted, and Albert ceased to be a citizen of Württemberg, the German state where he had previously belonged, and by extension, as a German citizen. Albert Einstein, formerly a German Jew, had now become stateless.

Mileva Maric

Mileva Maric, the woman who ended up becoming Einstein's lover, and subsequently, his wife, was the only female student in Einstein's class at the Zurich Polytechnic. She was also only the second woman in the

Department of Mathematics and Physics to complete a study program.

Mileva Maric was Serbian and had been in Zurich for two years by the time she met Einstein. She resided at Plattenstrasse, a location with numerous boarding houses, most of which were occupied by foreign students. Her residence was just a few minutes' walk to the Polytechnic, which was also on Plattenstrasse. Born in 1875, Maric was four years older than Einstein; and ultimately, she was to die seven years before Einstein, in 1948.

In 1902, Einstein and Maric bore a daughter before they were married, whom they named Lieserl. It is not known what became of this daughter, and there are many different theories. Some sources believe she died at an early age, while others say she was given up for adoption.

In Zurich, Einstein took up residency in the same neighborhood as other foreign students. His rental room was on Unionstrasse. As soon as classes at the Polytechnic began in October 1896, Einstein and Mileva Maric struck up a friendship. They both had a lot of intellectual ideas to share, which strengthened their friendship. Besides sitting together during lectures, they would often meet at different places, including the library. By 1897, through 1898, Einstein visited Maric in her room, where they would compare lecture notes and share books. Although they moved cautiously where the relationship was concerned, they spent a lot of time together. They would also go for excursions in the Alps together, as they both liked and appreciated nature.

In time, Albert Einstein soon lost interest in the Winterler girl; he informed her of his intention to cut off correspondence with her. Marie Winteler was heartbroken. She suspected Einstein had gotten involved with another girl, which she later confirmed.

A Low Budget

While Maric resided in a boarding house owned by a man known as Johanna Bächtold during her stay in Zurich, Einstein at first stayed in a room in an apartment belonging to Frau Henriette Hagi, in Hottingen, a bourgeois district. He later shifted to a smaller place that was run by a woman known as Stephanie Markwalder. During the four years he studied at the Polytechnic, Einstein depended on the 100 Swiss Francs his maternal aunt granted him every month.

Zurich Polytechnic Lecturers

While in Zurich, Einstein took up a teaching program; however, he had not abandoned his quest for physics. Although Einstein did not explain the reasons for his choosing teaching at Zurich Polytechnic, it is quite likely that he wanted to establish a middle ground between what he had wanted to do and what his father had wanted for him. The reason his father had preferred electrical engineering was that it was easy to earn an income, either through formal employment, or as an entrepreneur. With teaching, Einstein may have thought, it would be easy for him to secure a job as well as to support the family now that his father's business had failed.

Einstein also liked the fact that he could pursue his favorite subjects, such as physics and mathematics, thus quenching his thirst for academics, even as he sorted out the practical issue of making a livelihood.

Professor Weber

Einstein studied a lot on his own and had come to admire the works of different scientists, including those of Heinrich Friedrich Weber, a lecturer who would become one of Einstein's instructors at Zurich. Weber's area of specialization was electrical engineering. At the Polytechnic, Einstein would spend a lot of time in Professor Weber's laboratory studying his favorite subject, physics. Weber was also the head of physics at Zurich Polytechnic.

However, Einstein gradually realized that Weber's approach was outdated; he was stuck on the discoveries of the 1850s. When it came to electricity and magnetism, Weber did not want to hear of anything outside the works of Helmholtz, the German scientist. As a student who took a creative approach, Einstein was frustrated with Professor Weber's views and attitude.

Einstein could not understand why an enlightened individual such as Weber would ignore the different brilliant work of those such as James Clerk Maxwell.

Einstein was particularly interested in Maxwell's theory of electromagnetic fields, which was more modern than the theories Weber valued. Einstein would also dig deep into an article written by Heinrich Hertz which discussed Maxwell's theory, entitled, "Über die Grundgleichungen der Elektrodynamik für bewegte Körper," or "About the Basic Equations of Electrodynamics for Moving Bodies."

As he had at an early age, Einstein continued his private study. Not only did he read serious works by Maxwell, but he also read works of great scientists, such as Gustav Robert Kirchoff, a German physicist, Heinrich Hertz, also a German physicist, Hermann Ludwig Ferdinand von Helmholtz, who was a German physicist and a physician, as well as other contemporary physicists.

Hermann Minkowski, who was Einstein's mathematics lecturer, was very helpful to Einstein during his studies at Zurich Polytechnic. Even after Einstein had left the Polytechnic, Minkowski still proved to be of great help. He was particularly instrumental in devising a mathematical system which supported Albert Einstein's Theory of Relativity.

Drab Lectures

In due time, Einstein soon began playing truant, missing Weber's classes and those of Professor Jean Pernet, opting instead to read on his own. In preparation for major exams, he would rely on notes from his close friend, Marcel Grossman. Grossman was the son of a Zurich factory owner, who had been exposed to a liberal environment that Einstein admired.

Einstein quickly fell out of favor with his two professors, Weber and Pernet. He was even reprimanded by the administration, for not behaving as expected as a student. Not surprisingly, his performance was not impressive when it came to subjects taught by the two professors. He even scored notoriously low marks in his third year when the class was tested on a beginners' course.

Owing to the toxic relationship that had developed between Einstein and these professors, especially Weber, the Polytechnic did not offer him an assistant's job, as they did all the other graduates in Weber's class.

Marcel Grossman and Michele Angelo Besso

Although his circle of friends in Zurich was quite small, the friends he made were dear to him, as well as very helpful, even in his later life. Marcel Grossman, whose specialization was mathematics, was one of those friends. In fact, he helped Einstein to secure the Patent Office job in Bern after he had lost the Polytechnic opportunities. Later, when Einstein was seriously working on his scientific papers, Grossman also helped Einstein with the mathematical aspects of the General Theory of Relativity.

Michele Angelo Besso was another great friend of Einstein's. He was a mechanical engineer based in Zurich, whom Einstein had met while playing violin with a Zurich-based amateur music group. Einstein would join the group on Saturday afternoons during his stay in Zurich. Besso was a great support for Einstein, encouraging him to read works by Ernst Mach, an Austrian philosopher, who held contemporary views. The philosopher's views and attitudes, particularly his empirical positivism, as well as the distrust he had in metaphysical speculation, ended up having a great impact on Einstein, to the extent of impacting his theory of special relativity.

Chapter 9: Before and During WWII

As is clear from the behavior of Albert Einstein and the actions he took throughout his life, he had changed from a quiet personality in childhood, to a bold, and sometimes, rebellious, adult. He also socialized well.

Although he had relinquished his German citizenship when he was preparing to move to Zurich, he was still willing to return to Germany, his birthplace. He had been stateless for five years by the time he acquired Swiss citizenship, in 1901, the same year that he received his diploma in teaching from Zurich Polytechnic. He was to retain that citizenship to the end of his life.

Although he could not at first get a teaching job in Zurich, he was later to receive a Ph.D. from the University of Zurich, in 1905. This was the year popularly known as Einstein's miracle year, the year he published four scientific papers and drew the attention of academia. He was only 26 years old.

Einstein and Maric had married only two years before, in 1903, and the following year they had a son, who was born in Bern, and whom they named Hans Albert Einstein. They had a second son, in 1910, while in Zurich. The following year Einstein relocated to Prague with his young family because he had been given a job at the University of Prague. Einstein's stay at the University lasted only to 1912. He had been happy to take up a job that had previously been held by a physics professor, who had retired and left before the university could find a replacement. He would have stayed longer at Prague were it not for his wife's insistence that they leave. Apparently Maric was not all happy in Prague.

Divorce

By April 1914, the Einsteins were back in Berlin. However, Mileva Maric Einstein soon discovered that her husband was seriously romantically involved with his cousin, Elsa Löwenthal. Maric packed her bags, took their sons, and departed for Zurich. The couple remained separated for five years, formally divorcing in February 1919.

That same year, Elsa and Einstein married. Their close personal relationship dated back to 1912. Einstein was prepared to settle in Germany, teaching and pursuing his passion, which was scientific research. In 1919, Einstein bought a piece of land in Capruth, a tiny village near Berlin, where he hoped he would retreat to clear his head and relax, after spending days at the university where life was hectic, and for the most part, oppressive.

Caltech

Einstein soon received an invitation to teach at the California Institute of Technology (CaItech) on a temporary basis. He took the three month job, despite the fact that Robert Millikan, the Nobel Prize winning physicist associated with the institution, had been highly critical of Einstein's public agitation for human rights. Einstein left Berlin for a U.S. job for the first time in December 1930.

While in the U.S. Einstein met Edwin Hubble, the astronomer, and learned about his telescope project, which he was working on in Pasadena, California. By March 1931, Einstein was back in Germany. This time he spent a lot of his time in Capruth, at his county home, where he continued working.

Oxford

In May 1931, Einstein and his wife again traveled to the U.K. Having received an invitation to join the staff of the University of Oxford, his lecturer's job had a five year contract. Nevertheless, Einstein was only obligated to be at the university, at Christ Church, a small amount of time each year.

Because of his duties at the university and his personal pursuits, Einstein often found himself spending a lot of his time either in Pasadena, or at Oxford. Even will all the free time he had at his disposal, however, Einstein did not bother to travel to Germany. He was happy instead to be far away, avoiding the anti-Semitism that had begun to spread in Germany, as well as the political tensions that had begun to build.

Although Einstein appreciated the job opportunity he had at Oxford, he did not stay as long as it had been hoped. Things changed when he met Abraham Flexner, an eminent American educationalist. Einstein learned that Flexner had received funding to facilitate construction of a science research institute of international standards at Princeton, New Jersey.

Through Flexner's initiative, Einstein was invited to join the Princeton fraternity as a member of teaching staff in 1933, which he obliged. To his thinking, Einstein would not stay at Princeton full time, but would instead spend half of his time in Berlin. However, he soon ended foregoing Berlin. On January 30, 1933, Adolf Hitler took over power in Germany. Hitler belonged to the National Socialist Party that was not only anti-Semitic, but was also zealously anti-intellectual. Einstein knew at once the Nazi regime was his enemy.

Einstein's fears about the Nazi regime were soon realized. The German government froze his bank account and seized his Capruth home during his absence. Einstein had known Hitler's government would be no good for the Jewish people, but he probably did not anticipate that the regime would move so fast. Einstein decided to act swiftly too, to do what he needed to do to end his relationship with Germany. He did not see how he would ever return to a country that had shown so much hatred towards him.

Einstein left the U.S. and traveled to Europe, from where he wrote a resignation letter to the Prussian Academy of Sciences, Germany's most prestigious academic society, which had very exclusive membership. He publicly declared he no longer had ties with Germany, and showed total opposition to the government's so-called National Socialism. That same year, he and his wife immigrated to the U.S. where he was later to take up citizenship.

1933–1940

The rise in 1933 of Adolf Hitler to power made Einstein's life a nightmare. The fact that he was of Jewish descent and a scholar placed him in a terrible situation. And then there was also the issue of his personality that added fuel to an already volatile situation.

As aforementioned, Einstein was vocal in the face of worldly injustices, and this only served to make him the enemies of oppressors and their cohorts alike. It had not been lost on the so-called German nationalists how vocal Einstein had been in the fight against injustices in other parts of the world, especially the U.S., so when the Nazis took over Germany, Einstein easily made their list of marked men.

However, it was also painful for Einstein to have to leave his post at the Berlin Academy of Sciences because not only did he earn a living while there, but he was also able to advance his scientific study and research. Taking up American citizenship, as he did in 1940, only underlined the finality with which he had bid his motherland goodbye.

Hitler's regime began to torment Einstein by, as aforementioned, seizing his property and freezing his bank account, a sign that worse things were in store for him if Hitler's people were ever to lay hands on him.

Then illness struck. In 1935, doctors diagnosed his wife, Elsa, with serious heart and kidney ailments, and in

December of the following year she died. Einstein was once more alone.

As he continued to learn of Hitler's atrocities back in Germany, Einstein began to reevaluate the position he had always held with regards to trying to sort out political grievances through war. His stance had always been that nothing warranted a country sending its troops to war against another, or for people taking up arms against a regime, no matter how tyrant. The behavior of the Nazis, however, made Einstein change his position. He would, in fact, have done anything to see Hitler's regime toppled and the Nazis crushed.

It is, therefore, not surprising that, in 1939, Einstein accepted an invitation from the U.S. Navy when WWII broke out, to take up a position that required him to handle the evaluation and approval of new weapon plans.

During WWII, Germany, Italy, and Japan fought on one side against Einstein's new host country, America, which fought alongside the Soviet Union, Britain, Canada, Australia, France, New Zealand, China, and India. It could not have been a happy experience for Einstein, considering that he had relatives, friends, and colleagues in Germany. He could only have consoled himself with the reminder that these were extraordinary circumstances that justified taking up extraordinary measures.

Einstein was to cast his pacifistic views aside to proactively help his host country. Einstein's nuclear physicist friend, Leo Szilard, who was of Hungarian descent, when he heard Einstein's fears that Germany would not hesitate to create a nuclear bomb, urged Einstein to communicate his fears to the U.S. President, Franklin Roosevelt, in writing. Szilard wanted to see the U.S. to accelerate any plans the country may have had for creating nuclear weapons, and Einstein agreed. After all, Einstein had gotten word that scientists in Germany could make an atomic bomb. Still, having been a pacifist all his life, Einstein did not avoid inner turmoil.

In fact, Einstein's response to the U.S. bombing of Hiroshima and Nagasaki confirms the pain he experienced, as he had changed his position to embrace weapons of mass destruction, only to witness indiscriminate deaths among innocent civilians, while the regimes of terror were still in place.

During the years after WWII, Einstein campaigned to have countries dispose of their nuclear weapons, especially as a member of the Emergency Committee of Atomic Scientists. This organization took it upon itself to educate the public about the dangers of atomic weapons, with a view to getting the public to put pressure on their governments to be responsible in the decisions they made pertaining to such weapons. In short, the bitter reality of WWII reinforced Einstein's earlier stance as a pacifist, and thus he became a strong proponent of nuclear disarmament as well as international cooperation.

Chapter 10: Prague

Einstein was truly a global citizen. While born and raised in Germany, he began traveling at an early age. The first time he had traveled a significant distance without his family was at the age of 16, when he abandoned secondary school in Germany to join his family in Italy.

Einstein soon left his family behind and went to Zurich of his own volition, to pursue his love for physics. Even after completing his studies in Switzerland, he still continued to travel, to the U.K., the U.S., and other countries. Prague was just one of the cities Einstein lived in for a time.

To use the words Einstein spoke in 1911, the city of Prague was "wonderful" and "beautiful." Currently, Prague is the capital of the Czech Republic. Einstein was a resident of the city from 1911, to 1912. As he described his stay in Prague, it was the place that accorded him the tranquil environment to ponder over the General Theory of Relativity, and to formulate it in a definable way.

Prague College, where Einstein worked, was variously a home to other renowned personages. These included Karl IV, the Holy Roman Empire Emperor, who was its founder; Arnost von Pardubice, the archbishop who was the college's first director; and even Tycho Brahe, who was a royal astronomer, a man dedicated in the search for God, and a great scholar.

Other famous personages who had held a teaching job at Prague included Kepler, who served as the royal clock maker; and Joost Buergi, the mathematician credited with inventing logarithms; Bernhard Bolzano, a philosopher who was also a theologian; and Christian Doppler, the famous physicist, among others.

Highly Regarded

When Einstein was offered his job at Prague, it was as if destiny were on his side. He was chosen from a group that included two other lecturers, winning the job in his absence.

Einstein had begun his teaching profession in 1908, having served as a patent clerk in Zurich immediately after college. When it came to teaching, it was the University of Bern that gave him his first teaching job when he was engaged as a private lecturer. Then, in 1909, the University of Zurich gave him a job to teach theoretical physics. Soon, he was to proceed to the University of Prague.

A vacancy at Prague had come up when the professor of theoretical physics at the university, Hofrat Ferdinand Lippich, retired. Hofrat simply means that he was a civil servant, who had been conferred an honorary degree. Lippich had left the university, and the position remained vacant. It was then that Mathematician, Georg Pick, the faculty head, together with Dean Anton Lampa, a faculty member in philosophy, began the process of searching for Lippich's replacement. The three candidates they recommended were Dr. Albert

Einstein, Professor Gustav Jaumann, and Emil Kohl. Gustav was at the Technical College at the time, while Emil was a university lecturer in Vienna. When the names reached the Vienna Ministry of Culture and Education, which had the final say, Einstein was the obvious choice.

At the time, Bohemia, the part of Austria where the German University of Prague was located, belonged to the Austro-Hungarian Empire. The university was later to be made part of Charles University, considered the oldest university in the Czech Republic. It was also the first university in all of Central Europe.

As for Einstein's recruitment, administrative negotiations began, and all seemed fine, until it came to the final stage where Einstein was to be sworn in, according to the norms of the institution. The big question was: How was he going to swear allegiance to the institution and its ideals when he was an atheist? The reason everyone took Einstein to be an atheist is that he had formally declared himself undenominational when he was in Zurich. Now, that self-proclamation had come back to affect him adversely.

Since Einstein had to undergo the requisite imperial ceremony, so he could take up the job he had been offered, he was not going to let his religious status get in the way of his taking an oath. He therefore declared himself a mosaic. Mosaicism was a belief system adhered to by an ancient Jewish sect.

Thus Mosaic is what Einstein filled in the space meant for religion on the reception form. Of course, in fact, he did not practice anything Jewish, ancient or modern, and he had not even undergone a Bar Mitzvah; however, that was irrelevant to him. In any case, he did not see what the protocol had to do with his commitment to teaching physics at the institution. However, as much as he detested red tape, he wanted the job, and he knew the requirement to formally declare his religion, or denomination, was not personal. Therefore, on April 1, 1911, Einstein took the oath of office and began his teaching job at the University of Prague.

When the Institute for Theoretical Physics was opened by Minister's decree around the same time Einstein was recruited at the University of Prague, he was also given the position of managing it.

At the University of Prague, Einstein was a full professor of Theoretical Physics. He was soon called upon by the monarchy to seek Austrian nationality. He was also required to don the gala uniform, which consisted of a black coat with golden ribbons, a rapier, and tricorn. All this ceremony, to Einstein, was just laughable, as writer Johannes Wickert notes in his monograph on Einstein. However, again, Einstein wanted the job, so he kept his amusement to himself.

Family in Prague

By the time Einstein joined the University of Prague, he was 31 years old. His wife, Mileva Maric, who was five years older than him, was 36. They had brought their two young sons with them to Prague, Hans Albert, who was seven, and Eduard, then only a year old.

The family occupied a newly built three bedroom flat in Smichow, a district in Prague. The flat, which even had electricity, was on Trebížského Street, no. 1215/7, which was renamed Lesnická Street in 1947. In those days, living in a building that had electricity was a novelty. That house in which Einstein and his family lived has been marked for historical purposes, complete with a life-size sculpture of the professor's head. It also bears a plaque indicating the dates when Einstein lived in the house.

There is also a street within Prague 10 that the administration named after Albert Einstein in 1971. The street is close to others that have been named in memory of other prominent scientists.

The area was panoramic at the time and a great site for a man such as Einstein, who needed a serene environment in which to read and evaluate scientific theories and other intellectual matters. The Hradschin Panorama comprised the Karlsbruecke and the Kleinseitner palaces. The area was also inclusive of the old town, which had the town hall right in the middle, as well as the Altstaedter Ring.

The place was also considered the Jewish City. Three synagogues had been built where the old ghetto existed. Prague also prided itself in having four colleges, two of which were universities. The other two were technical colleges. These colleges were identified by race. Where Einstein taught, for example, was referred to as the German University.

The Einstein family did well in Prague, and like most professionals of the time, they had a maid. However, their living comfort did not diminish the sorrow that Einstein's wife felt. Around a half of the Jews living in the town were fluent in German, and everyone in Prague considered Einstein to be German. As such, he felt at home at Prague, and even moved around with confidence.

The case was different for Mileva Maric Einstein, who was Serbian by birth. She had spent a number of years in Zurich where she did not have to learn German. In Prague, she found it difficult to adapt and felt like an outsider. Although she had thought life would be interesting in Prague, it did not turn out to be that way for her. As the days went by, she became all the more sad, as arguments between she and her husband escalated. In short, she was in an unhappy marriage, living in a place she disliked.

Prague Jewish Community

To Einstein, it did not concern him whether a person was Jewish, Swiss, Dutch, or whatever other nationality. He was open to everyone. Back in Germany, he had no social concerns, even if he was of Jewish descent, and many people around him were native Germans – of course, until Hitler and his Nazis gained power.

In Aarau, while attending secondary school, Einstein was at home with the Wintelers and their friends, and he even made friends of his own, who were not necessarily of Jewish descent. He had settled nicely in Zurich, too, when in college, and there he also made friends of all kinds. Even his girlfriend, whom he later married, was neither Jewish nor German, but Serbian. And, of course, he was fine in Bern where he had lived among the Swiss.

Now that he was in Prague, there was also no reason for him not to feel comfortable. Instead, Prague offered more than he would have bargained for. There was a rich Jewish community in the town, and the people were excited to have him amongst them. He met with many socially when not at the university, and they shared many discussions, but Einstein paid more attention to those who were literarily and philosophically inclined.

It was at the salon, Bertha Fanta, situated on the Prague Altstaedter Ring, where the friends usually met. Before becoming a regular at the salon, Einstein would meet with friends at the pharmacy, Zum Einhorn. He had opportunity to meet members of the Music Society and members of the literary world, who lived in the old town that was predominantly Jewish.

Memorable people in Einstein's circle of friends at Prague included Max Brod and Franz Kafka, both writers, Hugo Bergmann, a zealous Zionist, Philipp Frank, a physicist, who later took up Einstein's position at the university after he left. Incidentally, they, too, loved music and were great debaters. They welcomed Einstein with open arms. He joined them in literary discussions as well as musical events.

Einstein was particularly fond of Professor Moriz Winternitz, and he enjoyed visiting the professor's family, which resided in the centre of Prague's old town. Winternitz, a scientist, was also an Ethnologist and Indologist. He was involved with religion, ethics, and language. In contrast, Einstein did not care about religion, and had no inclination for language. Nevertheless, the two scientists chose to ignore these differences and bonded on the issues they shared in common.

The two enjoyed round-table debates, where they would exchange ideas and opinions. Einstein was particularly happy that Professor Winterniz' sister-in-law, Ottilie Nagel, was a piano teacher. He was happy to bring his violin with him whenever the two joined the other friends.

Even as Einstein's social life was enjoyable, he did not let it interfere with his intellectual pursuits. Wherever he sat, he would register the physical nature of the room as well as ponder over the aspects of time, mass, and gravitation.

Teaching in Prague

As aforementioned, Einstein's teaching engagement as Professor of Theoretical Physics at Prague University became effective in April 1911. He began his first lessons during the summer, and he taught five days a week. On three of those days, Monday, Wednesday and Friday, Einstein taught Mechanics for one hour, beginning at 9:00 AM, to 10:00 PM. Then, for the remaining two days, Tuesday and Thursday, during the same hours, he taught select chapters on the Kinetic Heat Theory.

During Einstein's stay in Prague, he also organized two hour seminars at the Institute for Theoretical Physics. University classes were not large in those days, just as science classes are often not as large as the arts, and Einstein's class was no different. A few records indicate his class had 20 students, two of whom were female, but others indicate the class was much smaller, but of mixed gender. His annual salary was 8,872 Austro-Hungarian kroners.

It is worth noting that Einstein did not confine his teaching to the classroom. He also wanted to share knowledge with the wider community of Prague, and so he would organize public lectures where he would address large numbers of attendees at the auditorium.

Prolific at Prague

Einstein truly enjoyed his stay in Prague and worked hard. Nevertheless, he only stayed for 17 months at the university. In that relatively short time, Einstein produced eleven scientific works, five of which were on radiation mathematics and a Quantum Theory of Solids.

In March of 1916, his work entitled, The Foundation of the General Theory of Relativity, was published in Leipzig's Annalen der Physik, or Annals of Physics. In December Einstein's book, On the Special and General Theory of Relativity, was published. He later had the book translated to Czech, in honor of the people of the region who had shown him nothing but love.

Leaves Prague

Einstein ceased to work at the German University of Prague in mid-1912, after following the procedure for resigning. His resignation was officially accepted by Emperor Franz Joseph, and on July 25, 1912, Einstein and his family traveled to Zurich. The Swiss Technical College, popularly known as ETH, had nominated Einstein as full professor, and this made the move exciting for Einstein. His wife was even more thrilled to be leaving Prague, and more so to be returning to Zurich.

Einstein's fame and popularity as a brilliant physicist was soaring by now, and towards the end of 1913, he was elected a full member of the Prussian Academy of Sciences, which was based in Berlin. He had worked in Prague the longest, from 1914, to 1932, and his leaving had nothing with his experience at the university. It was instead the changing political atmosphere that had caused his departure.

Oxford University

When anti-Semitic sentiments began to spread across Germany, Oxford University quietly began to offer refuge to German Jews. Many Jewish academics, who found their stay in Germany unsafe, found sanctuary in Oxford. And Einstein was the most famous of the lot.

Oxford had awarded him a job in May 1931, and soon offered him a fellowship so he could study. His student status was meant to last five years, during which he would receive an annual stipend of £400 from the university. However, he did not remain in the Britain for the full five years, only for two.

During his stay in the U.K., from 1931, to 1933 Einstein was at Christ Church. However, as political changes continued in Germany, he began to get the feeling that Britain was not the best place to be. The dictator, Adolf Hitler, had risen to power in Germany, and his Nazi regime was spreading across Europe, and some in Britain shared their sentiments. However, to the British, Einstein was German.

Thus when Einstein saw an opportunity to work at Princeton in the U.S., and then there was actually a vacancy to work there, he did not hesitate to leave Oxford. He requested that his annual stipend be used to help other Jews who were in need; in particular, those fleeing the Nazi regime. Professor Frederick Lindemann, also a scientist, whose protégée Einstein had been while at Oxford, used the funds to help brilliant Jews escape the atrocious Nazi regime. Many of these beneficiaries of the stipend were scientists.

Lindemann, who was popularly referred to as the "Prof within Whitehall," later became famous for his role as Churchill's scientific advisor during the war. As for Einstein, he set a record as the first German scholar of Jewish descent to hold an academic position at Christ Church. Later, Einstein became a protégée of Viscount Cherwell.

During the 1930s, when anti-Semitism was rife, Lindemann traveled across Europe in search of Jewish academics. His aim was to offer them jobs at Oxford where they would be relatively safe from the Nazis and their sympathizers. Viscount Cherwell's travels are romanticized, as it has been said he traveled in a Rolls-Royce, while on the noble mission of rescuing Jewish academics. Other sources say he traveled in an Armstrong Siddeley.

Einstein at Oxford

Professor Lindemann, Cherwell, and others may have empathized with Einstein, seeing that Germany was wasting a great talent, but not everyone was happy that he had settled at Oxford.

In this same country that had provided a refuge for Jewish scientists, there were still voices that complained about such generosity. It was a gracious move for Henry White, Dean of Christ Church at the time, to offer Einstein a chance for a research studentship. However, as soon as word got out, J.G.C. Anderson, a Professor of Classical Art and Archaeology sent the dean a complaint letter, citing White's action as unpatriotic.

While Anderson had no complaints about Einstein's scholarly aptitude, White thought offering someone like Einstein a studentship was an act of supporting a German Jew. Thus the complaint was purely racial, and Anderson went even further to cynically point out that the emoluments such as those Einstein would be enjoying were not meant for foreigners when the college founders assigned them. Anderson curtly wrote that the university was running on a high government grant, and thus the college could not afford to subsidize a German's education and upkeep.

However, White did not take Anderson's criticism lying down. He responded that Einstein's achievements and reputation transcended national borders in their very magnitude. He noted that having Einstein as a student or member of staff should be the pride of any university.

Life at Oxford

Whereas many people speak of Albert Einstein as the scientist they have read about in history books, few are able to speak of things they learned from individuals close to them who interacted directly with Einstein. Andrew Robinson, an author who formerly worked as a newspaper editor, is one such person. His father gave him credible information regarding Einstein, having been a physicist himself, and who was also actively involved in scholarly scientific work during the same period as Einstein.

Robinson explains that his father, Neville Robinson, spent four decades at Oxford as a physicist, and he revered the scientific works of Einstein. According to the elder Robinson, in 1921, when the famous scientist paid a visit to England the first time, The Times only reported the visit in two sentences. They even described it as a private visit to see Dr. Lindemann of Wadham College, and that Einstein was given a tour of the main university buildings.

The same people who then did not give much weight to Einstein's visit saw him in a much different light years later, when Einstein was given an honorary degree from Oxford.

Oxford Host

Frederick Lindemann, under whose care Einstein settled in Oxford, had roots in Germany. Although he had spent virtually his entire life in Britain, and considered himself British, his place of birth was Germany. A few years younger than Einstein, he had been born in 1886. He returned to Germany when pursuing his Ph.D.

While in Berlin, Lindemann's supervisor organized an important scientific conference that was to be held in Brussels. That supervisor who set up the first Solvay

Congress was none other than Walther Nernst, who was later to win a Nobel Prize.

Nernst had appointed Lindemann to serve as one of his scientific secretaries during the conference, and it was there, in 1911, that Lindemann came into close contact with the young Einstein for the first time, as he gave a lecture on quantum theory. Needless to say, Lindemann would later to grow in academic and in social status, to the extent he even became a personal friend of Winston Churchill, the army officer who later became Prime Minister of the U.K.

More than a decade later, in 1927, Lindemann attempted to persuade Einstein to pay Oxford another visit to give some lectures. At the time, Lindemann had in mind the Rhodes Trust that had just been established, and on whose behalf he wanted Einstein to give lectures. Unfortunately, his efforts did not materialize. However, because Lindemann's scientific background that called for patience and persistence, he did not give up.

Three years later, in 1930, he tried again. This time, Einstein accepted Lindemann's invitation, but before long he had second thoughts. Lindemann then decided to use a different approach. He paid Einstein a visit in Berlin, and he also made his appeal through Einstein's wife, Elsa. The deal was sealed.

Einstein declared he would offer three lectures, and each would cover its own distinct topic, relativity, Cosmological Theory, and Unified Field Theory.

Prepared for Einstein to remain at Oxford for a number of weeks, Lindemann assured Mrs. Einstein in writing that he would take care of her husband, ensuring his time was well-spent and that he would not go astray.

Myths

As aforementioned, Albert Einstein was born German, was of Jewish descent, and, as most are aware, he lived to become a legend in the field of modern physics. He loved to play the violin, a skill he had learned early in age. He is also said to have had other attributes and preferences, some of which are plausible, such as being a romantic poet as well as an avid fisherman.

However, some things attributed to Einstein are just myths, and this chapter is dedicated to debunking some of the most common ones.

1. Myth: He was a poor student

The truth is Einstein was brilliant in school. He may not have scored as highly in the arts and languages as he did in science subjects and mathematics, but he certainly was not a dull student. Those who understand Einstein and the schools he attended believe this myth was initiated by people who had looked at his school reports from the Aargau Cantonal School. Aargau is the secondary school Einstein attended for a time in order to catch up on work he had missed out on when he prematurely left the Gymnasium in Berlin.

The school grading system was such that the highest grade was "1" (one) while the lowest was "6" (six). Since this was common knowledge, people who saw Einstein's report having a string of 6's thought he was doing very poorly, not recognizing that the grading system had actually been changed to read the reverse. As such, when Einstein's report form read 6 for a good number of subjects, including physics and mathematics, it meant he had scored the highest possible grade. In fact, in a report form that has been highly publicized, it is clear the lowest score he had was "4," which in itself was a pass.

Another point that proponents of the myth that the famous physicist was dull in school flaunt is the fact he failed the entrance examination to the Swiss Polytechnic. The circumstances, however, for those who understand them, do not warrant the conclusion that Einstein was a poor student.

When Einstein took the exam, he was underage, barely 16 years old. At the same time, he was subjecting himself to an examination meant for secondary school graduates, when he had not yet completed his secondary school course. And because of the fact that he had not done too poorly on the exam, the physics professor at Zurich Polytechnic advised him to stay on in the country to prepare for a second attempt after completing his secondary school course.

2. Myth: He had Asperger's Syndrome

Einstein may have kept to himself early in age, but that is not necessarily because he naturally shunned the idea of being in a social situation. He had a speech problem that would have led any person to avoid situations that demanded he speak a lot. It is clear as his ability to speak improved, that he related well to other people and was happy to exchange ideas.

What is notable is that he was keen to pursue friendships that enriched his passion; people who helped him to understand physics and related issues better. He would not have received books from his uncle and reading material from other people in the absence of clear communication and a reasonable degree of social interaction.

For those who believe that Einstein often being on his own as a reason to say he had Asperger's Syndrome, what they fail to consider is that it is difficult to solve intellectual problems, especially of those of the nature Einstein dealt with, in noisy and rowdy social circles, or even in calm discussions and dealing with different topics.

After graduating from college and entering the job market, it is clear Einstein traveled to many countries within only a few years, more than most people travel in their lifetime. When he wrote about his travels, he detailed close interactions he had had with other physicists, as well as other people outside his academic field. These are experiences that would be unlikely for someone who had Asperger's syndrome. In any case, none of his friends or relatives ever suggested he had the condition.

People with Asperger's Syndrome not only tend to be anti-social, but they also tend to be obsessive about one thing. For Albert Einstein, physics was his thing, yes, but he did not pursue physics to the exclusion of all other things. A look at how passionately he engaged in the fight against racial discrimination is sufficient to show the scientist did not have Asperger's Syndrome. And even when it comes to the field he so much loved, he did not just dedicate himself to scientific discoveries, but he also went to class and spoke to the community to discuss his theories and findings.

3. Myth: Einstein was a vegetarian

In general terms, a vegetarian is someone who has chosen not to eat meat. The reality was that Einstein began to avoid meat when he started having stomach problems, mainly of a digestive nature. He would experience intestinal pains, ulcers, jaundice, and his gall bladder would be inflamed. That was even before he was 50 years old. Due to those medical problems, his doctor advised him to stop eating meat. And he did, for his health.

The reason some people may have thought he was a vegetarian by choice, was the fact he was sometimes seen as empathizing with vegetarians. He concurred with the general premise of which vegetarians became averse to consuming meat, and he is even noted to have admitted feeling a sense of guilt as he ate meat, but he did not reach a point of making the decision to keep off meat on moral grounds. In short, Einstein was liberal with what he ate, until health problems set in.

4. Myth: Einstein bears responsibility for bombing Japan

To allege that Albert Einstein was the cause Japan was bombed, is to say that the U.S. would not have created an atomic bomb were it not for Einstein; this is entirely inaccurate. It is true, however, that his research and scholarly findings helped the scientists who created the atomic bomb. However, the U.S. was already discussing the possibility of building nuclear devices before the threat of WWII.

It is true that at some point Einstein said something encouraging about the U.S. making an atomic bomb, but it was in form of a letter, allegedly written by his friend scientist, Leó Szilárd, but signed by Einstein, to tell President Roosevelt that there was need to accelerate the research on nuclear weapons because there was a credible potential threat from the Germans. It should be noted it had come to Einstein's knowledge that some German scientists had succeeded in the most crucial scientific step needed to build a nuclear weapon.

Einstein, with firsthand knowledge of how evil Hitler's regime was, felt inclined to warn the president. Einstein believed Hitler could go on an indiscriminate bombing spree once he had the wherewithal to make atomic bombs. Beyond this piece of advice Einstein provided in good faith, he played no other role in the making of the atomic bomb. The U.S. security forces ensured he did not go anywhere near the laboratories where work related to making the bomb was taking place. They either did not trust Einstein entirely, his being originally German, or they felt uncomfortable working intimately with a person who had manifested pacifist ideals. Whatever the reason, Einstein was denied access to Manhattan Project, the actual bomb-making project U.S. scientists worked on in liaison with U.S. army intelligence.

5. Myth: Einstein was left-handed

While the scientist is shown in photographs pointing, beckoning, writing, and making other spontaneous moves with the right hand, some people just have the belief that that left-handed people are unique in a good way. This need to mythologize Einstein as one of a kind likely led to this myth.

6. Myth: Mileva Maric partnered with Einstein in his scientific discoveries

The fact that both Einstein and his first wife, Mileva Maric, were in the same department in college means they could have discussed academic matters. In fact, it is documented that they had shared a lot of time together at Zurich Polytechnic, as well as outside of class. Nevertheless, there is no credible evidence that Maric actively participated in the scientific study and formulation of the scientific theories Einstein came up with long after the two had separated.

6. Myth: Einstein was merely a theorist

The allegation that Einstein was solely a theorist, meaning he was not interested in the practicality of his work, is outright wrong. Many who think so rely on the fact that Einstein was not one to spend much time in a laboratory.

Instead, Einstein spent his time in areas where he felt his thought process would not be interfered with, and where he could make unbiased observations. In fact, there is more proof to debunk the myth that Einstein was a mere theorist. Could a theorist really invent practical objects such as a camera? However, Einstein has a list of practical inventions to his name, among them a self-adjusting camera; a silent refrigerator that was energy-efficient, and environmentally friendly; and even a kind of electromagnetic sound apparatus.

The fact that Einstein worked in a patent office and went on to involve himself in matters pertaining to patents is also a sign that he was a practical person, both within and outside of his field of science. For his work alone, he applied for around fifty patents in seven different countries. It is also notable that he gave testimony in courts of law between 1902 and 1909 when he worked at the Swiss Patent Office, standing in as an expert witness.

7. Myth: Einstein shied away from politics

If there is one scientist who rubbed political and academic administrations the wrong way, it was Albert

Einstein. People who shy away from being linked to certain political stances do not air their views publicly. In fact, if Einstein were to be compared to other scientists of his era, it would be seen he was the most vocal of them.

Einstein also spoke out against the oppression of African Americans. No one is going to work hand in hand and openly with the NAACP unless they are prepared to be political. In his famous Lincoln University speech about racial segregation, where he termed such discrimination a white man's disease, he boldly announced that he did not intend to be silent about it. Einstein did not avoid politics.

Even the fact that he turned down the post to be President of Israel when the state was formed had nothing to do with an aversion to politics. It was more about how good he thought he would be at it, as compared to the scientific work he was doing, and also about his passion in physics, which called for a lot of time and dedication.

Chapter 11: After 30th Birthday

In 1910, Einstein and his first wife, Mileva Maric, had their second son. They named the boy, Eduard. However, the child was born a during a period that Einstein and Maric were experiencing a strain in their relationship, something that probably put a dark cloud over the success Einstein was gaining in the field of science.

Not surprisingly, Einstein began a relationship with another woman; however, the woman he entered into a relationship with was his cousin. Her name was Elsa Löwenthal. After Einstein's divorce from his first wife, Mileva Maric, he married Elsa.

Besides the tension in Einstein's relationship with his first wife, there was also tension building up in the surrounding world, and soon the First World War (WWI) broke out. Surprisingly, it was at a time when many negative things were happening that Einstein succeeded in constructing the famous General Theory of Relativity, among the most valued scientific contributions of the twentieth century. WWI began in 1914, and in the thick of it, in 1915 Einstein introduced the theory to the scientific world and the world at large.

Within this theory, Einstein enabled his Special Theory of Relativity to be applied more broadly than it could initially be applied. He explained how closely related space and time are, and proved that they actually go hand in hand; hence calling the single element they formed, space-time. What remained was for Einstein, or any other scientist, to prove the theory right; and that it actually worked as Einstein had explained.

Einstein was great at thinking out how things worked, but proving them himself was often not so easy. His work can aptly be termed thought experiments, which fundamentally challenged science as it was generally understood; in other words, he challenged conventional science. What remained was for the General Theory of Relativity to be proven by way of experimentation as well as observation.

Soon, Sir Frank Watson Dyson was to conceive a way to evaluate the stars' apparent position with proximity to the sun. The uniqueness of this method was that it could only be applied when there was total solar eclipse, a very rare event. This is when the moon totally obstructs the light from the sun. The reason is that on ordinary days, the sun's light overshadows the one from the stars, so that the light from the stars appears obliterated. In short, it is not possible to locate the stars with the sun shining as strongly as it does.

General Theory of Relativity is Proven

After Einstein formulated the General Theory of Relativity, he seemed not to have had the tools to prove it. However, in 1919, Sir Arthur Eddington proved the theory true. As Einstein had asserted in his theory, in the absence of the sun's strong rays, the position of the stars would be different from where they normally appear. The time to watch that was during the eclipse. The reason, as Einstein had explained was that the gravity of the sun warps the space-time all around it, and in the process the path of the stars' light is bent. Of course, with the starlight's path bent the stars emitting the light would have their normal location apparently altered.

When Sir Arthur Eddington did his experiment, his observation supported Einstein's position in the General Theory of Relativity. And with Eddington's disclosure, Einstein instantly became a celebrity. The odd thing was Einstein's family liked that people liked Einstein's work, but they could not understand why all the fuss about him at that particular time.

Later on in life Einstein tried to explain to Eduard, his second born son, why he was famous, but that was only because Eduard had asked him. Einstein used a very basic explanation to explain to his son that he was famous because he happened to notice and acknowledge what other people seemed to have ignored, or to have failed to notice.

He had used the analogy of a blind beetle crawling on a curved branch. Although the surface on which the beetle is moving is curved, the beetle does not notice it. What Einstein had done to amaze everyone was that he had noticed something that was all along true, but people had not been able to see it until Einstein drew their attention to it.

Divorce

By coincidence, it was Einstein's year of greatest fame that the divorce proceedings between Einstein and his first wife, Maric, began. It was almost certain by then that Einstein was destined to win the Nobel Prize for Physics.

Einstein wanted to move on with his life, but apparently Maric was not yet ready to let him loose, although they had been separated for a number of years. Therefore, to entice her into signing the divorce papers, Einstein told her that all the money that would come with the Noble Prize would be hers for the taking, if he won it, which at the time seemed like a foregone conclusion.

Einstein's promise to his first wife in exchange for a divorce was a big deal, particularly considering the monetary size of the prize, as compared to Maric's annual salary. The prize money was 37 times the amount Maric Einstein earned in a whole year. Mileva Maric accepted her husband's offer, and consequently she signed the divorce papers.

Elsa

Four months after Maric had signed the papers and the divorce was finalized, Einstein and Elsa, his cousin with whom he had an affair with for seven years, got married. Einstein would have had a merged family were it not for the fact Maric had taken their two sons with her when she separated from Einstein and proceeded to stay in Zurich.

Elsa, for her part, had been married before and had two daughters. She had enjoyed a romantic relationship with Einstein for many years, but since she felt her reputation was at risk, she pressured Einstein into marrying her, which he did.

However, Einstein's divorce from Maric and his subsequent marriage to Elsa did was not monogamous. Einstein continued to philander at will. Still, his second wife stayed married to him, and only at death did they part, in 1936 when Elsa died of heart and kidney-related ailments.

The Nobel Prize

The first time Albert Einstein was nominated for Nobel Prize was in 1910, but he did not win at that time. He only won the coveted prize ten years later, in 1921. And, of course, he was actually not granted the prize the same year over the internal controversies within the panel. Instead, he ended up being granted the Nobel Prize for Physics the following year in 1922 at the same time that year's winner was receiving his.

Einstein's Nobel Prize for Physics was based on his breakthrough in Theoretical Physics, specifically for showing the principle along which a photoelectric effect takes place. It was the discovery of this photoelectric effect law that drastically changed the way physicists understood the way light behaves. In effect, therefore, it changed the way physicists looked at the natural behavior of the universe.

Contrary to what many people think, Albert Einstein's Nobel Prize in Physics was not based on his breakthrough relating to the theories of relativity. His different theories of relativity were very helpful to physicists and scientific work in general, but these were not the basis for his Nobel win.

Globe Trotting

Once Einstein had won the Nobel Prize, he became famous in academic circles. Different institutions wanted him to give lectures in their respective countries. He gave lectures in different parts of the world between 1921 and 1922, including the U.S., Japan, France, and Palestine, always welcomed by massive crowds.

Japanese Royal Family

Einstein had risen from a graduate that his former Polytechnic did not want on its staff, to a scientist of international fame and repute. When he traveled to Japan on one of his lecture tours, an opportunity arose for him to meet the country's emperor and his wife. The world had already termed him a genius, and everyone seemed proud to meet him, or, at least, to listen to him speak.

Unified Field Theory

Einstein did not sit on his laurels just because he had won the most coveted global prize. Soon, he started work on a unified field theory. Einstein was not always focused on developing theories. Earlier, he had worked with other scientists on quantum mechanics, and he had even participated in the advancement of that field. Nevertheless, he had branched out into the theory of physics, a field most scientists kept away from in preference for quantum mechanics.

He had found the theory of quantum mechanics incomplete, and therefore Einstein sought to find better explanations for scientific events, which would link the four important fields of magnetism, gravity, electricity, and quantum mechanics.

Unified Theory Took Seven Years

When Albert Einstein announced he had found the Unified Theory, the world was amazed. And so he was upbeat when, in 1929, he made public the gist of what he had discovered, findings that appeared in a Time Magazine publication in 1929. Einstein was actually featured on the cover of Time Magazine that year. He later appeared on the cover four more times.

However, Einstein's Unified Theory was not accepted by scientists of repute, who found deficiencies in it, and they let Einstein and the rest of the world know they were not satisfied with it. Einstein was thus to spend the rest of his life trying to seal the so-called loopholes, and to find a water-tight Unified Theory. Unfortunately, that did not seem to happen. It had even been said that some of equations he scribbled shortly before his death were an apparent attempt to further his scientific search for that theory. To date, no scientist seems to have found the grand theory Einstein sought for so long to no avail.

Germany

After Einstein's theory was published, the scientist tried to get away from the public limelight. He sought out a secluded part of Northeast Germany, the place where he spent his 50th birthday. Impressively, the city administration of Berlin granted Einstein rights to occupy a country house near the capital, which was located next to a lake. It was meant to be a birthday gift for the scientist from the city. Einstein was happy to receive the birthday gift, and he enjoyed sailing on the lake. However, he could not swim. However, enjoyable as his stay had been, Einstein's visit at the tranquil country house was short-lived.

The Nazi Regime

Albert Einstein had found a nice place to do his serious thinking, and to ponder over scientific events, an environment further suited to scientific discoveries. Unfortunately, Adolf Hitler's regime came to power in 1933, and soon Jews were being persecuted. Scholars, even as prestigious as they may have been for the country, were not spared as long as they had Jewish blood. Of course, Albert Einstein had Jewish blood, and his stay in Berlin, or anywhere else in Germany, was no longer tenable.

The country passed regulations in 1933, banning Jews from being holders of any official position, not just in politics, but also in academics, and all other areas. The immediate effect on Einstein, the famous scientist, was unemployment. Since he needed employment to be able sustain himself and his family, in addition to his other life pursuits, he immigrated to America. That was in 1933, when he was offered work at Princeton University.

Even as Einstein tried to secure employment for himself, he also tried to help out his fellow Jews. He wrote to different administrations and asked them to give refuge to German scientists of Jewish descent, whom Germany had suddenly rendered jobless. The letters Einstein sent to different countries are said to have saved more than 1,000 German Jews.

Once Einstein got to the U.S., he accepted his fate of being permanently displaced from his home country. As such, he applied to be granted a U.S. citizenship two years after his arrival in the country. In 1940, he received U.S. citizenship.

Civil Rights Advocate

Albert Einstein understood the agony of being the target of discrimination. As such, he could not hold his tongue when he came face to face with racial discrimination in the U.S. In New Jersey, he first witnessed blatant discrimination on the grounds of race and color. New Jersey had separate schools for African Americans and Whites. The same went for theatres. In a lecture he later gave at Lincoln University, Einstein did not mince his words when he termed racial discrimination abhorrent. He blatantly called it the worst disease Whites suffered from.

Einstein did all he could to get a platform to address racial discrimination. One of the things he did was befriend popular Black Americans, such as Paul Robeson, an actor. He also became friends with Mariam Anderson, an opera star. Moreover, he got himself associated with the NAACP, openly supporting their activities.

Nuclear Fission

As Einstein was proactive in learning about the scientific developments taking place in the world, he came to learn that some scientists in Germany had gotten a breakthrough that would enable them create a nuclear bomb. He had experienced the insensitivity of Germany's government of the day, and he believed Hitler would be glad to manufacture a bomb the soonest he had the wherewithal.

As such, Einstein, apparently prompted by a fellow scientist, decided to warn the U.S. before it was caught by surprise by Germany. He wrote the two-page letter often talked about that served to make the U.S.' nuclear project a priority. Although Einstein played catalyst, he neither got to be on the panel of scientists that created the bomb, nor did he set foot in the laboratories where the related work was going on. The Manhattan Project, the name given to the U.S. bomb making project, became a no-go zone for the famous scientist, who had nothing but good wishes for the U.S.

Apparently, U.S. intelligence did not trust him. While the reasons for such distrust were not disclosed to him, he probably linked them to the fact he had biological and historical ties with Germany, the U.S. nemesis. It is important to note that Germany had aligned itself with Japan and Italy in the looming war, which broke out a month after Einstein's warning to President Roosevelt.

Einstein's Letter to Roosevelt

Einstein's letter to the U.S. president regarding the need to accelerate work on nuclear weapons was dated August 2, 1939. He had wanted the U.S. to beat Germany in acquiring such deadly weapons.

In the letter, he explained to President Roosevelt how German scientists had managed to split the uranium atom, and how that feat would enable a nuclear chain reaction of great proportions. He explained to the president that such a reaction that involved uranium could easily become the basis for the manufacture of new types of bombs that were extremely powerful. In fact, he clearly said to the president that the discovery the German scientists had made could be used to help make an atomic bomb.

According to the knowledgeable and reputable scientist, one of those bombs, if created, would have the capacity to blow up an entire port and its surroundings. He explained to the president how Germany would have achieved that if they wanted. He said they would only need to load the deadly weapon of mass destruction onto a boat and ferry it to a port of their choice, from where they would explode it.

Einstein actually met the president in person thereafter, where he got an opportunity to explain his fears, and to share more information regarding the potential of bomb-making.

One reason that could support the premise Einstein did not actually make the U.S. create an atomic bomb was that it was not until two years after Einstein's leak about the discovery of the German scientists that America began related operations under the Manhattan Project, besides the fact he was not a part of the team that made the bomb.

Einstein was personally averse to war, and his talk about the need for the U.S. to urgently acquire nuclear weapons was to help, in his thinking, to avoid the potential devastation of parts of the world by the crazed Hitler. It could be said Einstein had settled on a lesser evil, and this can be supported by the fact he spent the rest of his life speaking against nuclear weapons and the need for a unified world. He is even on record as having later said he would never have advised the U.S. president to hasten making of nuclear weapons if he had any clue the Germans would not have managed to acquire some themselves.

He is quoted as having written that in his opinion, killing in war time is no better that killing at other times. In short, his stance was that it was evil to commit murder under any circumstances. No wonder in the list of things he vehemently spoke against, such as racism, was utilizing nuclear weapons for whatever reason.

That Einstein did not participate in making the atomic bomb, as valuable as his scientific knowledge might have been, is confirmed by the fact the Army intelligence never felt reassured enough to give him the necessary clearance to access the Manhattan Project. In fact, the attitude of the U.S. intelligence towards Einstein was even more unexpected, it was that of extreme caution. In fact, they prohibited the other scientists involved in the project from communicating with Einstein.

Vanities

Like most people, Albert Einstein was no saint. He had his vain side, and that included philandering. As aforementioned, he engaged in extramarital relationships, without appearing to be remorseful at any point.

He was also an ardent smoker, and in 1950, he received life membership at the Montreal Pipe Smokers' Club. As far as he was concerned, smoking a pipe calmed a person down and enhanced objective judgment for whatever sphere of human life he was considering. Unfortunately, Einstein's smoking affected his health negatively, and being the brilliant self and determined personality that he was, he finally heeded his doctor's advice and quit smoking.

The brilliant scientist retained one odd idiosyncrasy. Even after he had given up smoking, he would stick his pipe in the mouth, empty as it was, and just keep chewing at it. Whatever that did to his psychology, or his ability to remain steadfast in laying off nicotine is not known, but it made him feel good, and probably fought off anxiety. The person credited with noting this behavior of Einstein's was Roger Sherman, who served as Smithsonian associate curator of the Modern Physics collection.

Israeli Presidency

Einstein may have made enemies among the people who wanted to maintain the status quo in the world even where some people were considered lesser than others, but he also had his admirers. Some of his fans were actually politically powerful individuals.

When President Chaeim Weizmann of Israel died in 1952, the powers that be offered Albert Einstein the country's presidency, but he politely declined. He humbly explained he did not consider himself well-suited for the job because, as far as he was concerned, he lacked the political experience as well as natural aptitude to deal with people as required.

Although he could have been right in his self-judgment, it was also a reality that he was busy working with other highly-regarded physicists to understand the behavior of wormholes and black holes, and other abstract concepts that are still a focus of today's astrophysicists.

At Peace When He Died

Einstein is quoted as having said he was prepared to die if time was due, as he was satisfied with the role he had played in the world. On April 17, 1955, Einstein became ill. He had suffered an abdominal aortic aneurysm and was being attended at Princeton's University Medical Centre. He had declined any extraordinary measures to be taken to try and prolong his life, as he termed such move as tasteless. In his words, he wanted to pass away "elegantly." That same night, the revered scientist died peacefully in his sleep at the age of 76.

Einstein's Brain

Einstein was a scientist, and as would be expected, he was also a realist. Therefore, he believed he had an expiry date since he was made of matter, and he was prepared to embrace death. In the same breath, he did not want other people thinking of him as immortal or supernatural. As such, he asked that he be cremated when he died.

While his wishes were mostly fulfilled, the exception was the one relating to his brain. The pathologist in-charge, Thomas Harvey, extracted Einstein's brain, because he wanted it to be a subject of study. He was said to have diced it into 240 small pieces that would be used in different experiments.

Author, Brian Burrell, who penned Postcards from the Brain Museum indicated that Einstein did not wish to be held in such high esteem that his brain would be made a subject of study. He also did not wish for people to do things that appeared to be worshipping him.

In fact, according to Burrell, Einstein's instructions regarding how he wanted his body disposed of were very specific. He wanted it cremated and his ashes scattered secretly, so that the process would not attract the attention of idolaters. However, in the end, the preference of his fellow scientists carried the day. Einstein's brain was retrieved from Thomas Harvey and preserved at the Princeton University Medical Centre.

Chapter 12: Fans

There was more the famous physicist was admired for than science, hence the many fans he gained outside the field of science. Scientists found his scientific prowess unrivalled and the determination of his pursuits admirable. His formulation of the general theory of relativity, which ended up creating a revolution in the scientific field of physics, won him a multitude of scientific admirers. They aptly dubbed him Father of Modern Physics. They also considered him to be the physicist who had the greatest impact on science for the entire 20th century. His best renowned formula was his mass equals energy: $E=mc2$. It is arguably the world's most famous equation.

Without a doubt, receiving the Nobel Prize in Physics thrust Einstein into the limelight and won him more respect, while also expanding his fan base. The associated law of photoelectric effect for which he won the prize was fundamental in establishing the important position of Quantum Theory within the arena of physics.

Einstein's popularity transcends the field of science. In fact, many of the things that made, and continue to make, people generally admire Einstein as a man have to do with his personality and values.

Strong-Willed

Einstein was so humble that when questioned about his serious scientific theories, he casually stated that what the theories held was something so simple anyone could understand. In short, he was a great scholar and scientist, yet he tried to downplay his achievements. He was trying to disabuse the notion many people held that he was a genius. His oversimplified explanation was that he made a lot of headway in physics because he was curious, passionate, and reasonably imaginative.

In a bid to encourage budding scientists and other non-scientists, he explained that imagination and passion were more crucial to discoveries than plain knowledge. His position was that imagination was a better measure of intelligence than knowledge. He also held the conviction that experience was the best source of knowledge.

He had a uniquely imaginative view of life. He held the belief that not all things that one can count really count, and that not all things that count are actually countable. Overall, he took a simple view of life's happenings.

Einstein also believed in giving. He has been quoted as saying that life is worthwhile, only if it involves giving to others. Tired of the racial discrimination and unfairness prevalent in the world, he took the position that the people perpetrating evils were not the real threat to peace and equity, but those supposedly good people who remained indifferent as they watched evil deeds unleashed. That declaration was meant to be an instigation and encouragement to people of goodwill to stand up against dictatorial regimes and groups of people who perpetrated the evils of racial discrimination. Einstein is also reported to have said that while world leaders had facilitated different means of doing things, they had significantly mixed up and confused the intended ends.

When it came to the issue of imagination, Albert Einstein listed it highly on the list of priorities valuable to humankind. He termed logic as a quality surpassing logic in value. His simply analogy was that while one could follow logic to move correctly and conveniently from one point designated spot to another, imagination was better because it can help one move to any place the person chooses.

At a time when many people wanted to play safe, Einstein believed in invention; of course, invention which would be born out of creativity. He would note that fearing mistakes is a sure way to hinder one from attempting to create new things. In short, he believed the human race would get far if people stopped fearing making mistakes. This was a way of encouraging people to look at mistakes as events that could be learned from, rather than failures that called for condemnation. The creative and humorous mind that he was, he said that an intelligent fool was capable of making things bigger and even more complex, whereas a genius would make things less cumbersome and simpler to understand.

According to Einstein, being able to solve problems the way he did in science and math was not beyond the average person. One only needed to spend ample time trying to understand the nature of the problem and its root cause before proceeding to the stage of actual problem solving.

The example he gave to show what he meant was that with twenty hours to solve a particular problem, he would allocate eighteen of those hours to understanding that problem, and only two of them to devising the solution. Such standpoints made Einstein stand out as a great thinker. He also came across as a very humble individual, especially when he downplayed his intellectual prowess. He told people he did not think of himself as smart, but rather as someone who was persistent in whatever goal or issue he chose to pursue. Such humility certainly won people's hearts.

He was also not selfish with ideas. For instance, he would freely give advice on how to succeed in doing great things. He is known to have expressed his conviction that it was imperative one eliminated biases in order to find what the true position is, as opposed to seeing things in terms of one's expectations or preconceived ideas.

Another great piece of advice was that in order to solve a problem, one needed to summon a level of consciousness higher than that which brought about the problem in the first place. Something else which, at this juncture, might sound redundant is that this great scientist was a great advocate of change. That position earns him another category of admirers, people who feel gagged and restricted by stringent protocols within rigid regimes. As aforementioned, he himself disliked militaristic rules, something that is better appreciated after seeing how much he achieved in life just by being a nonconformist and his private scientific explorations.

Einstein won some people's hearts with his humor as well. For instance, he said that the clear difference between a fool and a genius was that while genius had limits, stupidity had none. He even famously said that the only two things that were infinite were the universe and stupidity of the human race, and he quipped that the former was even in question.

Of significance was how he tried to veil his unique abilities and intellect. In different forums he would tell people that the reason he appeared to creative was that he was discreet about his sources of information. Unlike a good number of people, Einstein admitted he was vain to some extent. In an explanation not devoid of humor, he observed that the more famous he became, the more stupid he became; a consequence he noted that was common with many famous people.

Einstein also has admirers from people who detest the conventional school systems. Many of those are brilliant people, who, despite their intelligence, are deemed misfits in the educational institutions that call for adherence to rigid rules and procedures. He failed to find much value in systems that taught hard facts and allowed no room for imagination and creativity.

For such systems, which are what existed in his time, he saw their products or graduates ending up with very little education, going by his definition of it. He said education is essentially what one remains after everything else one learned evaporates, or is forgotten. He even marveled at how some people were ever able to leave those institutions with any degree of curiosity left.

It is likely many can relate to Einstein's observation. Many of today's education systems are examination-oriented and restrictive in the modes of examination. As such, the bulk of those who pass the examinations are those who do well in reproducing facts. In the meantime, those who answer creatively but do not confine themselves to a set syllabus perform poorly or outright fail.

Chapter 13: Infidelity

As aforementioned, Einstein had a girlfriend, Maria, when he was at Aarau, Switzerland, the young daughter of the Winteler family that had hosted him while he was pursuing the remaining part of his secondary school education. Later, when he joined Zurich Polytechnic, he entered into a romantic relationship with Mileva Maric, a Serbian woman, with whom he studied, and who was five years older.

Subsequently, he discontinued his romantic involvement with the Winteler daughter. Of course that was not something that would have raised eyebrows, especially considering he was still not yet twenty and was experimenting with relationships before, presumably, settling on the one who would make a good wife.

However, it would not be realistic to use the word monogamy and Einstein in the same sentence. The scientist also famous for his pacifist stance found it difficult to remain loyal to one woman at a time. According to him, he did not philander with a view to injuring his partner's feelings. It was just meant to be. He expressed later in letters of how uniquely different he viewed romantic relationships.

Most Men and Some Women Cheat

When one of his female friends was devastated by her husband's cheating, on response, Einstein wrote to console her, and in the letter he asked the woman not to take her husband's cheating personally, since, as Einstein explained, cheating is normal for human beings. In short, Einstein's position was there was nothing odd for one spouse to cheat on another, whether it was the man or the woman. He told the female friend he hoped she knew that most men and a good number of women were not naturally talented in practicing monogamy.

He explained that people were generally prone to having affairs, and it was no good when anyone tried to resist the cheating urge. According to Einstein, any person forcing himself to observe monogamy only ended up causing bitterness to the parties involved. He explained that any proclivity, including that of remaining monogamous, was burdensome.

Moreover, when a man was trying too hard to remain faithful to one woman out of convention, he was likely to find himself torn between the two women involved, who had the potential to manifest hostility to each other just because of his involvement. What he concluded was that such situations are not easy to deal with for a well-meaning person. What is significant in this argument is that Einstein does not suggest that a man should try hard not to be caught up between two women. Instead, he has accepted that as a natural course of events, which, in his view, all parties involved should learn to live with.

In the letter to his friend, whom he was consoling, and which was originally in German, Einstein had gone further to explain that sooner, rather than later, nature would prevail, if individuals find themselves in an environment where they are continuously trying to resist pressure brought about by rigid conventions and circumstances. It would be correct to say Einstein was speaking from personal experience.

Even if his first romance as a teenager were to be put aside, there was still his serious relationship with Mileva Maric, whom he had met in Zurich. While their daily conflicts are not detailed, it was clear that their marriage bliss did not last many years. Einstein apparently began seeing his cousin, Elsa, not long after he was married to Maric. When Maric became too unhappy with their relationship, she took off to Zurich where she and her husband had first met, and she took her two children with her.

Without an iota of guilt, Einstein continued seeing his cousin romantically and married her as soon as his divorce from Maric was formalized. It actually appears Einstein had no qualms about continuing his relationship with Elsa as it was, without marrying her, but Elsa sought to salvage her respect by being officially wedded to him.

A Child Out of Wedlock

There is much evidence that living with a woman without marrying her was nothing Einstein found odd. He and Maric had lived as a couple long before marriage and had even given birth to a female child. As his biographer, Walter Isaacson, noted, Einstein was not in a hurry to formalize his relationship with Elsa after he and his first wife divorced. In a letter Einstein wrote in 1915, he explained to the recipient that the pressure to marry Elsa came from her parents, and that he considered their reasons to be based on vanity. He also added that moral prejudice was playing a role, as it was very prevalent amongst the older generation.

Einstein ended up securing a divorce from Mileva, not because he felt it was the right time to set her free after many years apart. It was instead to ensure that he would not be guilty of bigamy. Einstein was not one to feel as if he had tied Mileva down by not having a divorce processed earlier on. He did not believe in conventional rules. In fact, with Mileva, he was frank about the situation. He explained to her that his concern was about Elsa's two adult daughters, whom he said were likely to get their reputation hurt by the gossip surround their mother's romantic involvement with him.

Romantic Affairs

Once married to Elsa, Einstein clearly was not prepared to be devoted to her alone. Even when the two were officially married, he still had dalliances with other women. However, in his defense, Gerald Holton, a physicist who also happened to be science historian, explained in a 2006 Discover Magazine article that Einstein's behavior as far as relationships with women were concerned was nothing out of the ordinary. He averred it was typical of people of substance within Europe of that time, such as charismatic men with big names.

What made Einstein stand out in this behavior was his forthrightness. He did not pretend to be monogamous and faithful in his relationships. Instead, he tried to explain the scenario in which he found himself to be polygamous, and to try and create a moral code different from the one conventionally known. Over several years, Einstein's perspective of male-female relationships had become complex, and at the end he never bore any guilt for philandering.

Einstein's Imagination

Einstein has been quoted as having asserted that it is fine to do what one feels as long as their actions do not harm any other person. Apparently, Einstein embraced the free love that is practiced today before many in his days did. There are more than enough examples to affirm Einstein's open attitude towards romantic relationships. When he was still married to Elsa, for instance, he entered into a relationship with Betty Neumann, who was his secretary. He was so close to her that he even fantasized about her joining him and Elsa to live in the same big house, as his letters reflect.

Not surprisingly, Betty Neumann found that odd, if not ridiculous, and she declined Einstein's offer, even though it had sounded serious. In his response to Neumann's dismissal he quipped that she, definitely, had a better appreciation of the complexities of triangular geometry than he did.

Einstein also failed to show remorse when his wife, Elsa, found out her husband had had a fling with Ethel

Michanowski, who was her friend and a socialite in Berlin. He had flatly responded that it is all right for one to do as they pleased as long as they were not causing harm to anyone else. Evidently, Einstein's perception of male-female relationships was unique, seeing he could not fathom anyone getting hurt just because a partner strayed out of wedlock. He was contented that he still loved Elsa and wanted to remain married to her. To him, it was all that mattered and should matter to any woman, or man for that matter, whose spouse had flings while still in marriage.

Elsa's Daughter

In the 1930s, one of Elsa's children, an adult daughter, Margot, became concerned about the indiscreet philandering of her mother's husband. In an attempt to allay her fears that her mother may be hurt, Einstein wrote to her. In his letter, he did not deny what he knew was the truth. He explained that among the women he was romantically involved with, he was only attached to one woman, whom he referred to as Mrs. L, whom he said was decent and that he considered entirely harmless. Mrs. L., biographer Isaacson explained later, was an Austrian woman, Margarete Lebach.

For Einstein, casual sex affairs were not anything to worry anybody, not even for his spouse. He noted further in his letter to Margot that his affairs with other women hardly interfered with his feelings for her mother, Elsa. He was frank because he hoped to let her mother know that he still cared very much about her and that this reassurance would prevent her from getting upset with him.

Truly unconventional in his thinking, Einstein cherished his freedom, while being unhappy with any restrictions. To him, decency was not the way society viewed it. When one was in an extramarital affair and did not boast about it, he considered that to a sign of decency, solely because it kept the legal spouse from getting upset. However, he was not especially known for the indiscretion he took to be a mark of decency. His philandering, in fact, was common knowledge.

In a letter Einstein wrote to his second wife, Elsa, he seemed to challenge her to appreciate the decency of Mrs. M., another woman with whom he had been romantically involved. He pointed out the fact Mrs. M. had not bragged to Elsa about having been involved with her husband in order to keep her from getting hurt. Einstein then asked if Elsa would not consider such behavior irreproachable. According to Einstein, a wife should tolerate his husband's philandering if it did not affect other spheres of the couple's life, such as the husband taking care of and providing for her. His position was that a wife should be able to relate to her husband with a smile, even in the face of his unfaithfulness, and not be at odds with him because of it.

While it may seem as if Einstein was trying to defend the indefensible, his was a liberated view of things; this was the same attitude that made him despise stringent school rules and routine. However, it does not mean his attitude towards relationships worked in his favor. His first marriage failed even though he seemed to love Mileva Maric and the background they had in common as academics. His biographer, Isaacson, also noted that Einstein had a tendency to retreat into his comfort zone of science whenever he was confronted with other's emotional needs.

Chapter 14: Children

Many have wondered if Einstein's children inherited his genius. When addressing this question, it is important to understand what happens when a child is born of a brilliant parent, or even when both the child's parents are brilliant.

From an historical observation, if a child has a parent who is very brilliant, the child has a chance of inheriting those genes. In contrast, however, the child could just as easily inherit genes from the other parent who is only of average intelligence. However, in cases such as Einstein and his first wife, Mileva, who was also brilliant, their children had an even higher chance of inheriting exceptional intelligence.

Many experts have noted, however, that while children from especially intelligence parents often turn out bright, they often do not become as brilliant as their parents. This, experts say, follows the law of regression, where the children's brilliance tends to regress towards the mean. This essentially means that children of geniuses should not be expected to be geniuses as well; however, it is still reasonable to expect them to be bright.

Scientifically, the inheritability of I.Q. falls between 50% to over 70%. In some cases it has even been noted up to 90%. In the case of Einstein's descendants, they appear to have inherited his I.Q. to a noticeable degree.

Viewing Einstein's first wife as having been brilliant is not an overstatement, considering that she was with him in college at a time when many women did not enter into the male- dominated fields of science and mathematics. The pair did study together at Zurich Polytechnic, and also worked together during Einstein's search for scientific explanations and solutions.

For these reasons, one can surmise that Einstein's children turning out to have higher than average intelligence was a factor of both their parent's genes. The challenge that arises, however, when discussing the I.Q. of Einstein's children is that there was a lot of illness in the family.

Einstein and Mileva had three children, one of whom it is believed to have died in early childhood from illness, a girl only referred to in writing as Lieserl. Of course, there are some who have said the baby was given up for adoption instead; however, whatever really happened, it is not possible to evaluate the child's I.Q. without much information.

Einstein and his first wife, Maric, also had two boys, Eduard and Hans. Eduard was a medical student with promising prospects; however, at some point he was diagnosed with schizophrenia. Because of his medical condition, Eduard was sent to a medical institution where he spent a large part of his adult life. The treatment for patients with schizophrenia in those days was crude; therefore, Eduard Einstein did not fare well. Thus his cognitive abilities were compromised, and so an assessment of his I.Q. cannot be determined by his performance or achievements in life. However, the fact that he had qualified to train as medical student is a general indication that he was of higher intelligence.

As for Hans Albert Einstein, the eldest son, like his father, he proved to be a brilliant scientist, too, and became a hydraulic engineering professor at U.C. Berkeley. During his lifetime, he was also the world's greatest expert in the field of sediment transport. Clearly, although he did not become as distinguished as his father Albert Einstein or win a Nobel Prize, Hans was certainly very smart.

Hans' children, and Einstein's grandchildren, were unfortunately plagued with ailments. Hans had four children, and all but one died in childhood. The surviving son, Bernhard, he grew up to become a physicist.

Bernhard had pursued engineering like his father, and worked for Texas Instruments and Litton Industries. Like his grandfather, Einstein, Bernhard received a number of patents, at least six, in the U.S. His grandfather had received more patents in a range of countries, the U.S. included.

Chapter 15: Far East Travels

A man of the world, Einstein did not confine himself to Germany, his place of birth, even when his stay there was without going well. He also did not travel merely to take up jobs. Instead, he ventured out for a myriad of reasons that included meeting other scholars, giving lectures on physics, and as an activist, who motivated others into standing up for their rights.

When Einstein decided to travel to Japan, he was quoted as saying that he was taking the trip in order to escape the solitude he had been experiencing. He mentioned the 12 weeks he would spend at sea, starting from the month of October, and said they would provide some nice rest for him. It is therefore worth taking into account what had been happening in Einstein's life just before he took that trip.

In June 1922, his close friend, Walther Rathenau, who had been serving as Germany's Minister for Foreign Affairs had just been assassinated, an act that was believed to have been motivated by anti-Semitism. Not only had the unfortunate incident saddened Einstein, but it had also caused him great anxiety because he saw himself as another potential victim.

Towards the end of 1922 into the early 1923, Einstein went on a five and a half month trip that took him to the Far East, Palestine, and Spain. Einstein had decided to take up an invitation from the progressive Japanese journal, Kaizo, they had extended to him in September of 1921.

The journal wanted Einstein to give a lecture tour Japan, with a series on science for the capital, Tokyo, and six other lectures on other areas to be delivered in different cities. The journal offered Einstein £2,000 as an honorarium, which he had gladly accepted.

Japan in the Taisho Era

During the Meiji era, Japan was mainly focused on nation-building. At that time, the country's resources were directed to improving infrastructure and other systems. Einstein visited Japan later, during the Taisho era. By then, the country had embraced internationalism and democracy, as well as secularism and cosmopolitanism, in contrast to the parochialism of the earlier era.

Accompanied by his family, Einstein boarded the SS Maru and set off for Japan on October 8, 1922, when the ship left Marseille. The ship traveled via the Suez Canal. As aforementioned, Einstein was not a reclusive person; he was instead an observant person who appreciated his environment. On this trip, Einstein noted down in his diary what he saw along the way and the people whom he met. He also noted the activities of each day and the books he read while traveling on the steamer.

The Einstein family arrived in the Japanese city of Kobe after sailing for six weeks. Einstein had, presumably, relaxed a bit at sea, and he was looking forward to enjoying the new environment in Japan. The reality was that the Einstein family was not disappointed. The

Japanese welcomed them with open arms and made them feel at home. To make the trip even more fulfilling, large crowds turned up for Einstein's scheduled lectures. Einstein loved the enthusiasm he felt from the crowds that filled the auditoriums. When it came to the press, the Japanese media gave Einstein lengthy coverage, reporting on everything he said or did.

Kyoto Lecture

One of his most memorable lectures, Einstein delivered the Kyoto Lecture on December 14, 1922. The Kaizo Journal, which had issued the invitation to visit Japan to Einstein, published a few paragraphs that were contributed by Jun Ishiwara, a Japanese author. A Japanese publication, Einstein Kyoju Koenroku, published the contents of Einstein's lecture, which was published as a book in 1923, roughly a year after Einstein's trip to the country. As Ishiwara explained, Einstein spoke about his scientific journey which had culminated in the development of the theory of relativity. As Einstein reminisced on his experiences that had taken place years before the lecture, what he said made for rich material for both science historians and philosophers.

One important point that Einstein mention was that his theory had benefitted from the experiment done by Michelson, giving him insights into the principle on which he formulated the Theory of Relativity. According to Einstein, Michelson's experiment aided him before publishing the relativity paper entitled, On the Electrodynamics of Moving Bodies, in 1905.

Palestine

Einstein had harbored a wish to visit Palestine, mostly because he was eager to see the Jewish settlements built by the Jewish community there, locally referred to as Yishuv. The President of the day, Chaim Weizmann had, nevertheless, recommended that Einstein slow down on his visit, and not to treat it as a matter of urgency.

What Weizmann may not have realized was that Einstein had received an invitation from the Palestine Bureau Director, Arthur Ruppin. Ruppin had asked Einstein to visit the country for 10 days, and Einstein accepted the invitation. Shortly before leaving Berlin for Japan, Einstein communicated with Kurt Blumenfield, a German Zionist, informing him of the Palestine invitation.

In Palestine

The six week long stay the Einsteins had in Japan had been very gratifying. They left the Far East for Europe on December 29, 1922. After a month at sea, they reached Palestine, which was officially known as the British Mandate of Palestine. They spent 12 days there. Einstein was particularly happy to be able to travel locally, to see how the agricultural settlements were fairing, and what the big cities were like.

The Einsteins also had an opportunity to visit different educational institutions, as well as those that that dealt with matters of culture and the economy. They met some Arab dignitaries, who embraced them and made them feel welcome. It is important to mention that the Palestine the Einsteins visited in 1922 is today's Israel. As it happened, that famous visit remained the only one that Einstein was able to make to the area in his lifetime.

Spain

After leaving Palestine Einstein visited Spain in 1923, spending three weeks there, from February to March. Upon his arrival in Madrid, he was pleasantly surprised by the hero's welcome he was received. Oddly enough, while many knew Einstein was a celebrity, some had no idea why.

An amusing anecdote, which Thomas F. Glick, a U.S. historian, has noted survives of a chestnut vendor on the streets of Madrid, who recognized Einstein's face and yelled blessings in excitement, praying for God to grant a long life to the automobile inventor.

The highlights of Einstein's visit to Spain in 1923 included lectures he delivered in Barcelona, Madrid, and Zaragoza. During the weeks Einstein spent in Spain, he was the central focus of conversation in most social circles.

Chapter 16: The FBI

Usually, when a person is under the surveillance of the Federal Bureau of Investigation (FBI), it is easy to assume that the person is a risk to the country, particular prominent individuals, or even someone in the community at large. Many, who are under FBI surveillance, it could be said, may potentially cause harm in some way, such as treason. However, there are some individuals who are entirely harmless but who do not appear to be so; therefore, they remain in the FBI's files in anticipation that one day their assumed covert transgressions will be discovered. Such was the case with Albert Einstein, the world famous scientist. As it happens, the FBI kept him under surveillance until the day he died.

Of course, Einstein was harmless when it came to overthrowing a government or causing injury to others. However, his liberal attitude towards issues and openness of expression often made those in authority uncomfortable. As aforementioned, beginning from when he was a teenager he was resistant to rules, procedures, and rigid routines.

For instance, when Einstein remained behind at Luitpold Gymnasium in Germany, as his family went to Italy, Einstein presumably wanted to complete his secondary school course, just as much as his parents wanted him to do so. However, he was soon overwhelmed by his dislike for the rigid rules he was subjected to at the Catholic school, especially so because his parents were not around to encourage him to continue. To everyone's surprise, he abandoned school before completing his courses and left the country in 1894 to follow his parents.

Had Einstein's parents not understood him so well, they may have thought he was under some external influence, from either some bad company or others, who did not want the young Einstein to gain a solid education. It also helped Einstein that he did not just rebel without a plan. He left Luitpold with the aim of asking his parents to sponsor him to a college of his choice; one that would enable him pursue his preferred course, and which involved subjects he enjoyed and was good at, such as science and mathematics.

To the ordinary observer it might appear as if the young Einstein was presumptuous, believing his parents would do his bidding and enroll him to a college of his choice, especially when he had abandoned a reputable school in Berlin. He may have even appeared to have been conceited, assuming he would succeed in life, without having to attend rigid school systems, which, in his view, were run like military camps.

Fortunately, Einstein was neither presumptuous, nor conceited. He was aware, however, that he was more demanding than other children, and that his shift from Berlin to some otherwise apparent limbo would make his parents uncomfortable. With this in mind, Einstein went to Pavia equipped with his complaints about Luitpold. He also went to his parents with a well thought out plan of action. Einstein wanted to join the Zurich Polytechnic in Switzerland. He had done his due diligence, and so he knew the college had been established with the aim of producing scientists and engineers. And while he personally was crazy about science, his father wanted him to be an engineer for the practical reasons of earning a living. In short, he knew that given his selection of schools, convincing his father to sponsor him to Zurich Polytechnic would be relatively easy.

And so it was. This demonstrates that there were behaviors of Einstein's that only those close to him could explain, such as his parents, wives, and closest friends. In the case of his leaving Luitpold, some people may have considered that he had an aversion to education, which is not the case. If so, he certainly would not have proceeded to Aarau to complete the units missed in secondary school, of course, or trained as a teacher of physics at Zurich.

Some may have also seen the young Einstein's leaving Berlin as an inability to survive away from his parents. However, the reality is that Einstein was at ease living away from the family, as can is demonstrated by his stay with Professor Winteler's family in Aarau, as well as his comfortable stay in Zurich while training. Such misreading of Einstein's behavior is what led the FBI into placing him on its watch list. A question remains, however, about precisely what it was about Einstein's behavior that made it so the FBI kept him under their surveillance for the most of his life

Berlin before WWI

Einstein was busy enjoying his career in Zurich when Max Karl Ernst Ludwig Planck, popularly known as Max Planck, the 1918 Nobel Prize winner for Physics, together with Walther Hermann Nernst, or Walther Nernst, traveled to Zurich, with the aim of luring Einstein back to Berlin. After several attempts, Einstein finally accepted their invitation. On November 2, 1913, the German Emperor, Wilheim II, approved Einstein's membership into the Prussian Academy of Sciences.

Another offer on the table at the time was that of a professorship. Einstein accepted this as well and become a Professor at the University of Berlin, while not being obliged to teach. He was also later inducted into the Kaiser Wilhelm Institute for Physics that was yet to be established. After all the respect and honor bestowed upon Einstein by the Berliners, he moved back to Germany in April 1914, ready to take up his position in Berlin.

However, when WWI broke out, Einstein could not keep silent. Not even the risk of jeopardizing his job in Berlin would make him sit still when the war was going on that stood against his conscience. The war itself began on August 1, 1914, and not long after Einstein was expressing his anti-war sentiments.

Opposing WWI

Einstein was adamant about his pacifist stance. It is likely, just as Britain, Einstein saw WWI as an act of destruction that could have been avoided. Britain had urged some of the world's strongest countries to intervene in the conflict between Austria and Serbia, a conflict that was clearly drawing in other countries, such as Germany and Russia. It was evident the two were ready for a fight. The whole saga had been started by the incident where the Archduke Franz Ferdinand of Austria and his wife had been assassinated in Bosnia while visiting Sarajevo, by a person who was Austria assumed to be a Serbian nationalist. While Serbia was not defiant about this point, and instead proposed arbitration, Austria would not hear any of it.

Germany was quick to support Austria, which was already aligned with Hungary, and when Russia joined the alliance of Britain, France, and Italy, who sought a non-militant solution to the Austria-Serbia standoff, Germany was unhappy. It should be noted that in this period in history, Austria and Hungary operated together as a single empire.

When, on July 28, the Austro-Hungarian Empire declared war on Serbia, and Russia, upon noticing Germany's support for Austria, warned Germany on July 29 not to join in the war, Germany became restless, particularly because it noticed Russia seemingly mobilizing its troops. Germany immediately warned Russia to stop mobilization. The Germans themselves, however, began to mobilize their troops, and by the time Austria attacked the capital of Serbia, Belgrade, both Russia and Germany were ready to step in, however, on opposing sides.

Things came to a head when on August 1, Germany declared war on Russia. From then on it was a series of combative declarations, with Germany declaring war on France as well on August 3, while invading Belgium that had remained largely neutral. Britain's declaration of war upon Germany then followed on August 4, for the reason that Germany had refused to heed Britain's warning to stop attacking Belgium.

Einstein was, of course, a very smart man and could see how a single event could have a dangerous, spiraling effect. This is why he held pacifist ideals for most of his life. In the case of WWI, since Britain at the time had a number of colonies, they were all presumed to hold the same stance as Britain. As such, Germany and the Austro-Hungarian Empire were, by extension, up against Canada, Australia, New Zealand, India, and South Africa, in addition to their initial rivals, Russia and France.

It was not only Einstein's colleagues who noticed his opposition to the war his country had entered into; his position was also noted by those who were influential politically, and this did not hold him in the good graces of the government. Countries normally expect undivided support from the citizenry when at war with external forces, and so even those who are hesitant to support the war are usually discreet about it. On the contrary, however, Einstein became one of only four prominent scholars who declared their outright opposition to the war, and who actually signed an anti-war manifesto. That manifesto not only condemned the war, but it went further to emphasize the need to have the European countries unite. Einstein even attended meetings organized by various pacifist groups.

Therefore, if the FBI thought that Einstein he was anti-American because he voiced his anti-discrimination ideals, and other such unifying principles, they likely also realized that his pacifist stance transcended geographical boundaries.

Einstein did not relent in his advocacy for fairness, even when he rose to such prominence as would have accorded him unique privileges. He became an instant international celebrity when the Nobel committee acknowledged his work in 1919, accepting him as a nominee for the physics prize. This was after his observations on how light bends and the impact that had on the position of an object had been validated with by observation during a total solar eclipse.

The validation of Einstein's General Theory of Relativity, by Sir Arthur Eddington, served to rewrite scientific laws related to space, gravity and time. This was a feat universally acknowledged as brilliant and monumental in its effects on science, and Einstein became well-known and admired. However, he continued to lend his name to organizations that advocated for peace and disarmament, and when he could and saw it as important to do so, he lent his presence as well.

Although the U.S. remained neutral in WWI, when other countries were forming alliances in the war, it does not mean that the country was anti-war at its core.

As was evident in WWII, the country had no qualms decimating Hiroshima and Nagasaki with atomic bombs in a bid to crush its opponents. In short, even the U.S. expected loyalty from its residents, but for someone such as Einstein who had failed to support his home country in a time of war, many felt he could not be trusted. At the same time, the FBI thought Einstein kept in close contact with the German pacifist groups, and this warranted their surveillance.

WPC

The FBI did not also lose sight of the fact that Einstein's support for anti-war groups and his ownership to being a pacifist inspired the Woman's Patriot Corporation (WPC) to pen a complaint letter to the government. The group felt the rising mood of feminism might jeopardize a woman's position in the home as far as man being the breadwinner was concerned. The sixteen page letter that advocated that Einstein be denied residence in the U.S. pointed out that the anarchic-communist groups he was affiliated with were really too close for comfort; and that even Stalin, the Russian dictator, was not affiliated with as many. The letter even alleged that the scientist was a pernicious influence, who was intent on shattering the military systems of established governments. The U.S., wishing to be a global military power, could not ignore such threats, and this is one reason the letter from the WPC letter made the top of the list in the FBI file on Einstein.

Fortunately, for Einstein, the FBI did not take action that would have led to him being barred from the U.S., although though they did continue to surveille him. Even as Einstein took up his job at the Institute for Advanced Study in Princeton in 1933, and the science world monitored him to note his professional achievements, the FBI also continued to monitor him on suspicion of being a potential threat to the U.S. government.

The FBI would have likely stopped monitoring Einstein when he got busy with his research and teaching; however, the radical scientist's attention was easily drawn to acts of discrimination and aggression that came to his notice. It seemed to touch a raw nerve, he would short circuit. For instance, in 1936, during the Spanish Civil War when there were so many atrocities being committed by the country's opposing forces, Einstein openly declared his support for Spanish groups that were opposed to fascism.

Why a scholar would speak on politics, and more so take a stand on matters involving the politics of another country, was beyond the comprehension of many, not least the FBI. If the U.S. had an opinion on the situation in Spain, it would be the government's role to express it, and not a university professor, the FBI may have reasoned, believing that Einstein was too political and radical for their comfort.

Even as Einstein dined with celebrities such as Chaplin, and human right activists such as Du Bois, or even as he spoke face to face with President Roosevelt and other senior politicians, Einstein could not have failed to have sensed a hidden eye focusing on him. However,

Einstein being who he was, a man of conviction as well as a bold realist, he did not allow the opinions and attitudes of others to dictate his lifestyle. He continued instead to pursue his scientific research and to give lectures, and he continued having fun as well. Just because the FBI was spying on him, it did not mean either that would stop him from having dalliances with other women, married or otherwise.

In its defense, the FBI had received numerous tips that pointed to issues of Einstein's loyalty to the U.S., and the possibility he could be a threat to the country's security. An institution such as the FBI cannot be expected to dismiss such warnings, as ridiculous to some may be, until they had good reason to clear a subject of suspicion. With Einstein, every time issues likely to raise suspicion cooled down, he would soon do something else that was likely to again raise questions where his loyalties lay in the eyes of the conservatives.

A Russian Spy and Hollywood

Some tips that had been provided to the FBI by undisclosed sources labeled Einstein a Russian spy. Of course, he must have been happy when Russia cautioned Germany about attacking the empire of Austro-Hungary, but that did not really qualify him to be a supporter of the Russian regime and its policies in entirety. And even if he had admired Russia's socialist agenda, it would not automatically make him a Russian spy. However, that appeared to have been at least one premise for which the FBI had monitored him, the allegation that had served as a Russian spy while living in Berlin.

Other reasons that made the FBI see Einstein as a threat to national security included his support for Civil Rights activists, his open declaration that he advocated pacifism, as well as his socialist ideals. In fact, some people went further to spread odd rumors, which, nevertheless, threatened the status quo. One such ridiculous rumor was that Einstein was in a communist conspiracy that was intent on taking over Hollywood. How Hollywood became an FBI issue is not clear; however, it is obvious that established government institutions do not like it when there is someone or something threatening the established order of things.

The issue of the FBI mistrusting Einstein to the extent of monitoring his moves and speeches is not just speculation. Long after his death, information relating to Einstein linked to the FBI surfaced. In 1983, for instance, Dr. Richard Alan Schwartz, a Florida International University of Miami Professor of English, had his hands on an FBI file relating to Einstein that was 1,427 pages long. Although it was a censored, Dr. Schwartz could not miss some information that would interest the public, and thus he disclosed it in The Nation magazine.

Since then, more credible information has surfaced, confirming that the FBI really thought Professor Einstein was not to be trusted as a friend of the U.S. Fred Jerome, a renowned journalist, who had an inclination for science, once liaised with the Public

Citizen Litigation Group in suing the U.S. government to try and force it to authorize the release of a less-censored copy of FBI's file on Einstein. Jerome was interested in establishing the truth about why the FBI monitored Einstein's activities, and where the bureau got its information, with a view to including the information in a book he was planning to publish.

According to information extracted from the FBI file, agents secretly rummaged through Einstein's trash, and also monitored his mail. They also monitored calls made to him, as well as those that he made. According to Jerome, who had time to screen through the file, the activities of the FBI, as far as monitoring Einstein was concerned, seemed to have become routine. He says it appeared as if all they embarked on when they got up every morning, besides brushing their teeth, was to open other's mail and tap phones.

As far as the records go, the FBI did not find anything tangible which they could pin on Einstein to have him deported. Still, they continued to spy on him, a routine that continued religiously until the good scientist died in 1955. It appears the bureau was so desperate to find anything unpatriotic against Einstein that they had even cooperated with the Immigration and Naturalization Service in an investigation to evaluate if they could deport him.

It should not be surprising that Jerome worked to force the release of Einstein's file. Jerome had a communist father, and so he had firsthand experience of how it feels to have the FBI cast a shadow on their target. His father, who was an official of the Communist Party, had been imprisoned for three years, courtesy of the Smith Act, which criminalized the act of advocating for overthrow of the U.S. government.

Jerome had reported on the Civil Rights movement as a young journalist, and later on he proceeded to teach and serve as a media consultant. He was the founder of the Media Resource Center, an institution that links journalists with scientists. From what he learned from his research on Albert Einstein, Jerome contends the scientist was astute in championing the right of the underdog and was politically savvy. He notes that Einstein actually scrutinized the organizations he was going to associate with and support, meaning that he did not just join protests easily. Overall, Jerome's work disabuses the notion that Einstein was an ignorant idealist.

There were other activities and people that Einstein associated with that contributed to the FBI's suspicion about him. His liaison with Paul Robeson, the actor, as aforementioned, was one. Some, the FBI included, could not understand how a privileged intellectual such as Einstein could support a rally that had been organized by Robeson in 1946, which protested lynching. Einstein did not belong to the threatened groups, and the fact he had been given a safe haven by the U.S. should, in their reasoning, make him a supporter of the status quo. Clearly, he was not.

At the same time, after WWII, Einstein was very vocal about the horror of the atomic bomb and the unnecessary destruction of the war in general. He voiced his dream for a universal government, where there would be no borders to fight about to expand territories, and enemy countries to fight against. As Jerome notes, Einstein the scientist, was not politically ignorant. He acknowledged the fact that a universal government also had a potential to become tyrannical, and he feared such an eventuality, but he said what he feared even more was the potential for another massive war, or even any wars.

Among the anti-government moves the FBI may have taken into account was the appeal Einstein had made for Julius and Ethel Rosenberg, a man and wife who had been sentenced to death by a U.S. court for espionage. Einstein had also discouraged anyone from testifying before the anti-communist sub-committee headed by Senator Joseph McCarthy.

The Case of the Rosenbergs

The case against the Rosenbergs was a sensational one and cannot easily be forgotten in the history of the U.S. The couple was condemned for leaking secrets related to the atomic bomb to the Soviet Union, as WWII was underway.

It is common knowledge that the U.S. had manufactured its atomic bombs in an environment of high secrecy and security. Even the Nobel Prize winning scientist, Einstein, was denied access to the bomb-making project. At the same time, the U.S. having the bomb-making knowhow, while the rest of the world, presumably, did not, put the U.S. ahead in terms of national security. Even if they did not manufacture other bombs, it would still be enough to use an advantage to threaten other countries to keep out of U.S. territory. As such, having its own citizens expose the secret was unforgiveable; hence, the Rosenbergs received the death penalty. The charge against the Rosenbergs had been espionage, and they were taken to the gallows in 1953.

At the time, the Rosenbergs were not the only individuals associated with leaking bomb-related secrets to the Soviet Union. However, they were found to have been the masterminds; therefore, they received the ultimate penalty.

The beginning of the trail was Klaus Fuchs, a British citizen. In February 1950, the FBI, working with British authorities, gathered enough evidence to convict Fuchs. Fuchs had worked on the process of bomb-making both in England and the U.S. during WWII, and so he had very sensitive information at his disposal the entire time. When he was accused of passing top secret information to a foreign country and knew the grave consequences he was about to face, he owned up to it, but added that he was just a pawn in the whole game, and that there were others involved.

Fuchs named Harry Gold, an American, as the person who served as the courier. Once the information was ready, Gold was the individual who would safely relay it to Soviet agents. On receiving this crucial disclosure from Great Britain, the U.S. got hold of Gold and began interrogating him. Knowing what the consequences would be, such as Fuchs, Gold decided to talk. Gold's crucial disclosure was that a young man, David Greenglass, was the greatest source of information, and that he had been more involved in the conspiracy to leak the information than Gold or Fuchs. Greenglass had worked in the bomb manufacturing laboratory, and when captured and interrogated, he admitted that he had been involved in letting out sensitive U.S. secrets relating to the making, handling, and use of atomic bombs. However, in this conspiracy, most importantly, he had superiors.

Greenglass named his superiors, who happened to be his own sister and her husband. Greenglass' sister and brother-in-law were the brains behind the historic espionage. Politically, they were extreme leftists. Even before WWII, they had been very vocal on matters of labor in the U.S., and other issues of a political nature, especially in the period beginning the late 1930s. While the U.S. authorities captured Julius in July 1950, his wife was arrested the following month. Unlike in today's courts where lawyers can have the case drag on for eternity through dubious injunctions and appeals, the Rosenberg trial took less than a month. The duo was charged on March 6, 1950, and the jury convicted them on March 29, 1950 for the crime of conspiring to commit espionage.

In such a high profile case, most are very cautious about aligning themselves with the culprits, lest they, too, are seen as condoning the crime. This was not the case with Professor Einstein, however. Although he personally would not have leaked such sensitive information to anyone, let alone the Russians, he lobbied for the Rosenbergs to be pardoned. Hence, he made national headlines by appealing for a pardon for the Russian spies who, in everyone else's eyes, had betrayed the U.S.

Einstein's position on the Rosenbergs was difficult for the FBI to ignore. Since there was a senate hearing about the case in the U. S., Einstein even discouraged potential witnesses from testifying. This was another way of frustrating Senator Joseph McCarthy's sub-committee. For a person such as Einstein, to whom the U.S. had played a good host, it was easy to see his actions as a betrayal. To the FBI and like-minded people, Einstein must have taken that stance with an ulterior motive. However, in reality, Einstein was a scholar who had noticed early what many other people came to notice much later, that McCarthy and his team were quick to label people as communist, which to the U.S. equaled an enemy.

At the same time, Einstein may have been among people who held varying views regarding the leaking of the secrets of the atomic bomb, who also felt the crime should not have been classified as serious as it was, considering that the information had already been passed on to a country that fought as a U.S. ally, and not as its enemy in WWII, at the time the information was shared.

Authorities

According to a prominent historian, Dr. Robert Schulmann, Einstein made authorities uneasy, so much so that many would rather not have him around if they had a choice. With such a reputation, it is not surprising that the FBI would have been interested in watching Einstein's ways. In any case, the general consensus then was that liberalism was the gateway to communism. However, in reality, Einstein was never one to adhere to mass systems, or to owe them allegiance. He seemed instead to be one to judge an issue on its own basis per the prevailing circumstances, as opposed to supporting an issue because of some doctrine or convention.

One person who tried to explain why, in his opinion, the FBI followed Einstein was Dr. Ellen Schrecker, a Yeshiva University historian, and the author of No Ivory Tower, McCarthyism and the Universities. Her contention was that the FBI saw a man whose values seem to be leaning left, and to them that meant that he was dangerous.

A fellow historian, Dr. Richard Gid Powers, concurred, saying the whole scenario was crazy, but the FBI seems not to have had a choice. Taking into consideration all the propaganda the Soviet Union was spreading across the world, luminaries such as Picasso, Charlie Chaplin, and Einstein, who vehemently criticized U.S. policy, especially after WWII, had to be watched closely, as they were making worse the U.S. position in the world arena. To Dr. Powers, the U.S. and the Soviet Union were engaged in a high stakes propaganda game, and the U.S. was eager to prune any sellouts, if there were any. Dr. Powers worked at the College of Staten Island and the Graduate Center of the City University of New York. He also authored Secrecy and Power: The Life of J. Edgar Hoover. According to Dr. Powers, the U.S. was facing a set of brilliant people too smart to engage in an argument, and so the best the FB could do was just to keep watching them.

Chapter 17: Fascism

Einstein was a man of letters, with a science-oriented mind, and much as he cared little about politics, he just could not withstand the Nazi regime. When a regime practices fascism, as the Nazis did, it means it does not care about the interests of individuals, but it rather looks at the people as one mass unit that should be given rules and regulations to live by for the benefit of its benefactor, the government.

The regime works under the premise the leadership knows what is best for the people, and so it goes ahead to design and implement policies as it deems fit. That was the situation that befell Germany, when, in September 1930, the country went into national elections and raised the previously dreaded Nazi Party to power. These were the first national elections held in the country since the 1929 economic crash that began in the U.S. Germany had experienced some tough times on its own, not only because it had incurred destruction and losses in WWI, but also because it had liabilities, such as the payments imposed on it by the Treaty of Versailles for war reparations. This was the agreement made among WWI allies, which specified where German borders were to be and how much Germany was going to pay for initiating and exacerbating WWI.

Germany had declared its surrender formally on November 11, 1918, and the Treaty of Versailles went into effect on June 28, 1919. Germany was a signatory to the treaty, although it was not party to the decisions taken by the allies, Britain, Russia, Italy and France.

When Germany was unable to pay France the requisite reparations, France moved into German territory and took over the Ruhr Valley, an area where German industrialization was at its best. This placed Germany in an even worse position; however, the U.S., which had opted to remain neutral in the war, came to Germany's rescue.

With money lent by the U.S., Germany met its obligations as stipulated in the treaty of Versailles, and it proceeded to rejuvenate its economy. In the meantime, the German chancellor had managed to convince France to withdraw from German territory. Germany's economy did well from 1924 onwards, until the effects of the crash came about in 1929. In short, the Nazi regime rose to power around a year after the start of economic turmoil, a time when masses were vulnerable and susceptible to political manipulation. After the war, an interim government of the Weimar Republic, the German territory, held power.

Hitler was influential in the party win, especially because he was a great orator. The party, which then went by the less-threatening title of the National Socialist German Workers' Party, had won by 6,400,000 votes, clinching 107 seats in the Reichstag, or the German parliament. After this big win, the name, Nazi, seemed to be sanitized, and most generally embraced the party's leadership.

Hitler's Vulnerability

It should be mentioned that from the onset that Einstein had little, if any, admiration for the way German politics were conducted. He preferred to be indifferent to whole political arena, but that, too, meant there was a good deal he also did not comprehend about the relationship between the masses and the people aspiring to lead them.

When Hitler came to power, Einstein predicted his reign would be short-lived. Therefore, although Hitler's rise to prominence was generally too fast for comfort, Einstein did not seem to read much deeper into the reasons for that. He swept it aside lightly, saying it only confirmed how poor German's body politic was. The closest he came to blaming Hitler was alleging, and rightly so, that Hitler had manipulated the people with the promise of a better economic environment.

Einstein was asked in December 1930 what his opinion was on the Nazi regime, and his response was that Hitler would be out as soon as the country's economic state improved, as the only reason people seemed to embrace him was that they were surviving on empty stomachs. While addressing a Jewish organization, he reiterated the need to continue Jewish solidarity, but pointed out there was no good in expressing dissatisfaction regarding the election results. Incidentally, Einstein was not the only one who erred on the fragility of Hitler's tenure. Other Germans did as well.

The people of Germany were eager to have their economy thriving again, but that was not what Hitler was mostly concerned about. He wanted the German military back to where it had been before the war, or even improved. He wanted the military armed to the teeth. After the war, the German military had been left with only 100,000 men and a small number of heavy weapons. It lacked an Air Force and the Versailles Treaty prevented it from building one, just as it demanded a limited tonnage of warships. To Hitler, those were requirements on paper only, and he did not intend to adhere to them. Hitler's attitude towards war soon put him at loggerheads with that of Einstein, the pacifist.

Pressure on the Government

Einstein may have remained indifferent, as more enlightened people jostled for political office, but when it came to Germany's efforts to accumulate armaments in apparent preparation for major war, he could just not watch and do nothing. Besides his pacifist ideals, the country had only had a decade of relative peace, during which people had tried to rebuild their lives.

Einstein thus began to communicate with like-minded people in a bid to avert the direction Germany and other European countries appeared to be taking, which generally indicated war. He tried to instigate a mass rebellion against forced military service that he himself had evaded in his youth. His was pacifist politics at its most intense. Einstein even wrote to a London movement, No More War, at the beginning of 1928, expressing his contention that when countries are at peace, they are obliged to ensure they do not take any action whatsoever that would lead them to war.

As days went by, Einstein felt more ill at ease as far as the potential for war was concerned, and in 1929, he expressed his feelings in writing, indicating it was up to the people to ensure that their government did not lead them to the slaughterhouse of war ever again. The days that followed brought even more misery for Einstein, because as 1930 drew close, all indication was that many European countries were geared towards preparing themselves for the eventuality of war.

In short, diplomacy was not being given any chance whatsoever, and in desperation, Einstein declared he had better "wait to be mutilated limb by limb, instead of participating in a war." He viewed war as an abomination that he could not stand to be part of. He actually termed it an "ugly business." One may wish to know exactly how much impact Einstein's pacifist campaign yielded, but he had given so much of himself emotionally that he soon tired. By the end of 1932, he had given up hope that the Germany he knew would survive economic hardship and kick the Nazi regime out that had systematically ruined daily lives.

Nazi Setbacks

In November 1932, when national elections took place, the Nazi Party lost a significant number of seats, and Einstein's friend, Kessler, believed the loss marked the start of the Nazi's exit. He was not alone in this thinking, as even astute political analysts thought the same. However, the party was given a new lease on life, not just by Hitler's persistence and determination to have controlling power, but also by the ridiculously stupid incompetence of Chancellor Franz von Papen.

The Chancellor had asked that Parliament be dissolved, when he realized the threat of a no-confidence motion against him was real. Of course, different political strategies took place thereafter, but to imagine that Papen, who was a member of the Catholic Center Party, could accept a coalition with the Nazis was unimaginable.

Hitler's Cabinet

As Einstein once noted, "the difference between wisdom and stupidity is that the latter has no limits." Chancellor Franz von Papen's move clearly supports Einstein's view. The Chancellor's action is what led to the formation of the Hitler Cabinet at the end of January 1933, and which later allowed him dictatorial powers, after the burning down of the Reichstag.

It came as a huge blow for Einstein to see the war-hungry party take power, when he had put so much effort into preaching peace, encouraging communities to demand it. He had not only addressed the issue at home, but also abroad. He had told his audiences it was disturbing to witness what he had, which was basically the collective surrender of a people to unreason. He had spoken to people, encouraged peace activists, written to organizations, and even raised money to support peace.

However, by the end of 1932, Einstein could not ignore the signs of doom.

He had learned from an early age to acknowledge when he was in a disadvantaged position, but it did not, nevertheless, stop Einstein from trying to advance his cause. That is precisely what he had been doing in trying to suppress the ascension of the Nazis to power. The personal effort was sometimes so overwhelming that he felt as if he were singularly trying to go against the world and he was sad for him whenever his efforts were defeated.

Einstein equated such an experience with one he had had at sea in 1931, while traveling to California, when the ship was faced with a storm. He noted in his diary entry how beautiful the expanse of the sea was, particularly when the rays of the sun fell on it, and how nice it felt to merge with nature. He also said he felt happy to realize how insignificant he was as an individual, although it was an unusual feeling. Of course, it was an unusual feeling, considering how much impact his scientific pursuits had had on the academic world at large, and the appreciation of an individual's limitation must be liberating. This shows that Einstein could easily shove aside any feelings of guilt that might creep in whenever the notion of failure set in.

Leaving Germany

On December 12, 1931 Einstein and his second wife, Elsa, boarded a train out of Berlin, and set out for the

U.S. As Einstein worried about the grim politics of his home country, Elsa was also worrying about her ailing daughter, Ilse. This was not one of the usual trips they had made when Einstein had been invited to give lectures, or to meet some prominent personalities, or even just for a visit.

As they had prepared to leave their home in Caputh, Einstein sensed they were looking at the home he had built for the last time, and he told his wife so. He had actually told her to look at the house closely, as she would never get a chance to see again. He obviously knew he had been marked for his agitation to oppose the laws of the land that the Nazis so much valued, such as military service for the youth, the accumulation of strong weapons, and an aggressive attitude towards other countries.

One thing that made Einstein stand out from his contemporaries was his readiness to adapt. He may have held strong beliefs about something, but if the world showed these were not plausible or workable, he revised his stance. Where politics were concerned, he had been all about morals and peaceable approaches for Germany. They had clearly not worked, as it appeared he had been trying to grind water with a pestle and mortar.

Nightmare

Einstein may have been too optimistic about the possibility of the German populace keeping the country out of the grip of fascists, but he certainly was not ignorant about the dangers of fascism. In his attempt to get some world forces to influence Germany for the better, he had traveled abroad several times in the early 1930s. One winter he had stayed at a bungalow along 707 S. Oakland Ave., in California, and in the subsequent two winters he had stayed at CaItech, where he worked as a guest professor.

Einstein's stay at CaItech raised the institution's standing, and although he always had his home country in the back of his mind, he still enjoyed his stay. He would travel in the region, giving lectures and making formal public appearances, in addition to his official work. All in all, he made a positive impact throughout greater Los Angeles, while he still reserved some hope that Germany might install a peace-loving regime.

It may seem as if it was mostly political talk for Einstein in the early 1930s, but that was not the case. He did his best to maintain a life of normalcy, even amidst the political anxiety in Germany. In March 1931 he had returned from a visit in the U.S. A month later, he visited England. His actual destination was Christ Church College, where he stayed for several weeks. His visit had nothing to do with politics or activism, but was purely professional. It was while he was there that he received an honorary doctorate degree (Dr. h. c.) of Science, conferred by the University of Oxford. He then returned to Germany to spend the summer at his home in Caputh, only to make another visit Pasadena, California, that December; these were the last of his days at his home in Germany.

In January 1933, when speaking at the Pasadena Civic Auditorium, Einstein pleaded with the U.S. to develop peaceful relations with his home country of Germany. Unfortunately, the reality he did not want to fathom came to pass, when in January 1933, Hitler officially became the Chancellor of the German Republic. It happened to be good luck that Einstein and his wife were already far away in Pasadena. On his ascent to power, Hitler and his party declared Einstein a persona non grata on German soil. As sad as the ban was, Einstein was grateful he and his family were out of danger, at least, overtly. His American friends empathized with him and treated him well. He even was able to make jokes. However, he still took some time to process the impact of the ban, and to ponder over his future. For a while, Einstein restrained himself from making any antagonistic statements against Germany.

Sly With Germany

Einstein was evidently not just brilliant in science. Even if no one had actually measured his I.Q., there still would be a wide consensus he was a brilliant man. He knew when to be confrontational, as well as when he stood to lose by being so. He also understood clearly that one may look cowardly one day, while strategizing to survive in readiness to fight another day.

In the early days of February 1933, he sent a letter to the Prussian Academy, where the community of scholars had honored and embraced him, asking to discuss the issue of his salary. He was trying to create the notion he was planning to resume normal work at the institution in the course of the year, but deep down he knew that was a mirage. In fact, that same day he sent a letter to Margarete Lenbach, his valued mistress, informing her he would not dare enter Germany because Hitler was a threat to him.

What Einstein had no clue about was that there were groups prepared to take action to show rebellion against the fascist regime, and this became clear to him when he learned that the Reichstag had been burnt down on February 27. This rebellious act in Berlin sent Hitler's soldiers on a rampage. They went all out to root out and crack down on presumed dissidents, the kind who supported Einstein's ideals. It was a field day for Hitler's bodyguards referred to as the SS, and his street fighters, those referred to as SA, to arrest and brutalize as many as possible who appeared to be possible threats to Hitler's regime.

A pamphlet that bore the names and pictures of perceived enemies of the state was printed and distributed all over the country. Not surprisingly, Einstein's name was on the list. The chilling part of that pamphlet that the administration kept reprinting is that under Einstein's photograph, was a caption indicating he was yet to be hanged. In short, Einstein's death sentence had been publicly declared without a legal trial.

As events in Germany unfolded, it became clear to Einstein he had been right to ask his wife to admire their home for the last time. There was no way they could safely return to Germany. After his great weeks in Pasadena, Einstein was set to travel to Belgium. However, a day before his departure, he decided to launch an attack on Germany from the place he felt relatively comfortable, Pasadena. All along he had followed the sad events taking place in his home country, and had only discussed them with family and friends. Now, he decided to make his stand known to all, the Nazi regime included.

Einstein declared publicly that as long as he was in control of his life, he would only live in a country that respected civil liberties, tolerance, as well as human equality. The long and short of his public declaration was that he would not go back to Germany because the country did not meet the conditions he had mentioned. It was another way of telling his fellow Germans and the world at large that he was at loggerheads with the Nazi regime and did not plan on returning to the country during its reign.

The Nazis Hit Back

Upon learning of Einstein's public attack on the Nazi regime, the government retaliated, publishing a rebuff of his charges, attacking him in exchange. The regime's criticisms of Einstein were published in the Völkicsher Beobachter, and other mainstream publications took up news. One carried a headline exclaiming how great the news was that Einstein was never to return to Germany. It continued to say how vain the scientist was, and how pitiable it was that he had the audacity to criticize the government from afar, when he actually knew nothing about what was taking place within the country. The publication went as far as claiming that Einstein had never been German to them, and alleging that Einstein considered himself a Jew.

Einstein both read and heard all the unwarranted criticism and pushed it aside. What he found difficult to bear was learning that his fellow scholars in Berlin had turned their back on him as well. He could not reconcile their behavior with the fact that they had been the ones who had gone all out to induct him into the Prussian Academy. He drafted his letter of resignation from his privileged membership of the academy while still at sea, and when he reached Belgium, he presented the letter to the German Embassy there. It was through the same office that he renounced his German citizenship.

Einstein Resigns

The Nazi regime was so bitter with Professor Einstein that they sought to humiliate him by forcing the Prussian Academy to expel him. To their shock and embarrassment, Einstein had beaten them at their own game. He had already tendered his resignation. They sought a way to punish him, and the one they found was through Einstein's colleagues in academia. The regime wanted them to denounce him, even in absentia, although he was no longer one of them. That was the directive issued by the minister in charge and academia heeded.

The stuff they published against Einstein was not befitting scholars of their status, but they did not seem to have much choice, considering they were under a brutal regime. The main statement declared that the Prussian Academy had no reason whatsoever to regret that Einstein had resigned, and that the academy was shocked that one of their own had decided to be confrontational with the government while on foreign ground.

Nevertheless, Einstein still had some loyal, sober, and bold friends, and one of them was Max von Laue. He was appalled that the respectable institution would succumb to pressure and issue such a statement. He had suggested that they do not do the minister's bidding, but when the issue was put to a vote he had the support of only one member among the fourteen others present. What was even more shocking was that a fellow Jew, Haber, who was also a close friend of Einstein's, also went along, agreeing to help mar Einstein's name. Haber's betraying Einstein was bad, but to Einstein, having Max Planck, a man whom he held with such high esteem to do so also, was disgrace to the scholar. Planck had, in fact, had head hunted Einstein for the Prussian Academy all the way in Zurich, but now that a political class had condemned him, Planck went along.

When the false allegations began to circulate in Germany, Einstein had even been gracious enough to write to Planck personally, where he explained that there was nothing defamatory about what he had said about Germany. Einstein pointed out that the allegation he was spreading rumors about Germany was false. He told Planck that the reason he had decided to speak out when he did was because he could sense the danger fellow Jews faced under the regime, and he was trying to avert the risk of their extermination.

It is likely Einstein expected Planck to be open-minded, and not to be biased, but clearly he was. In response to Einstein's letter, Planck said he could not see a situation where Jewishness and National Socialism went hand in hand. It was thus as if Einstein needed to deny his roots in order to fit in. Nevertheless, Planck continued to say that for him, he loathed both Jewishness and National Socialism, and that his loyalty was solely to Germany, irrespective of the reigning regime.

During the meeting to discuss Einstein's case at the academy, Planck had declared that Einstein had rendered his Academy membership untenable with his political behavior, and that he should not blame the German government for his exit.

Hitler's Thirst for War

As 1933 wore on, Einstein became more and more agitated about Hitler. He could not understand why the world was so quiet, when Hitler's thirst for war was so evident; at least to Einstein. For his part, Einstein decided he would do all he could to make people aware of Hitler's danger to his own people, and to others. He even paid a visit to Winston Churchill in September 1933, no longer concealing the fact he was in political exile. What Einstein realized was that Churchill had no reason to doubt him, only he did not see what he could be done about Hitler.

With every non-action, Einstein became all the more frustrated. In one interview, around the same time, he told his interviewer he could not comprehend how the entire civilized world could remain passive, while Hitler was manifesting clear signs of modern barbarism. He wondered aloud how if the world really could not read the signs that Hitler was trumpeting for war.

Abandoning Pacifism

As aforementioned, Einstein's position all along had been that there were different means of sorting out political problems, without resorting to war. However, after experiencing anti-Semitism in Germany and the adverse discrimination that rendered survival for Jews in Germany very difficult, he had gone out of his way to shout this reality to the world. Germany had shunned him, and the world turned a deaf ear.

The problem thus moved from being personal and racial, to being territorial. However, to Einstein's frustration, he seemed to be the only one who had a clear perception of Hitler's devious strategies. At last, he decided to spell it out loud and clear. In a statement he sent to The New York Times for publication, he explained that he used to believe that if he and others took a pacifist stance, there would be enough of them to keep countries from going to war. However, he had realized that circumstances could alter one's beliefs, and he was now declaring he did not want to remain a pacifist, at least not with the regime in Germany prepared to begin a war. And with that he proclaimed he was prepared to join military service if his services were required to save the European civilization that was clearly under threat.

The years 1939 and 1940 were Einstein's ultimate resolve to support military action to solve a human problem. By sending letters to President Roosevelt in connection with the making of nuclear weapons, he underlined his commitment to war.

Chapter 18: Idiosyncrasies

The winner of the 1920 Nobel Prize for Physics, Einstein was not a poor man by any standards. His salary from teaching and honorariums from various appearances and lectures were sufficient for him and his family to live a decent life. However, there were some behaviors he demonstrated that would have caused some confusion as to what his true economic, or social, status was.

For example, Einstein was extremely thrifty, wearing his shoes until they were completely worn. Herta Waldow, who served as the housekeeper for the Einsteins from 1927, to 1933, said the man always appeared to be out of money, and his wife could aptly be described as penny pinching.

The former housekeeper even noted that Einstein's favorite footwear happened to be sandals. It is not surprising, then, that one of his principles for which he hung a sign on the wall at Princeton stated that "not all that can be counted counts, and not all that counts can be counted." Still, even though this apparent thriftiness is an amusing idiosyncrasy, it could also show the man was not materialistic.

Einstein also could not care less about a modern barber. It was as if he wanted to extend his love for nature to his own being. He let his hair grow long, and when his second wife, Elsa, alerted him that a haircut was long overdue, he would just shrug it off. Finally, as a good wife who wanted her husband to be neat, she would pick up a pair of scissors and do the cutting herself. Einstein was fine with it. Einstein did not avoid the barber for lack of money or time. He just did not see why his looks should have been such a big deal. And since he loved Elsa, he sat still as she cut his hair short, peering at the size of it with her short sightedness. It is no wonder his photographs show a man with a funny looking crop of disheveled hair.

An Egg Man

According to Waldow, the great physicist never tired of eating eggs. The housekeeper would serve him fried eggs, and sometimes scrambled eggs, for breakfast, and that was virtually every day. Waldow has also explained that the eggs were sourced from a Jewish man, who was a bit elderly. Einstein would eat his eggs mostly with mushrooms, because he liked those too; it was the kind of thing he could have eaten three times a day without getting bored. Waldow said honey was Einstein's other favorite food item. He routinely purchased honey by the pail, directly from a beekeeper.

The man was no vegetarian, however, as some have suggested, but he surely did not want to see blood on his steak. He was insistent that his steak should be properly done. The rib tickling thing he said about bloody steak was that "he was no tiger."

He was also surprised to realize how much people hung onto his every word. He discovered this when he saw private remarks he had made published. Expressing his dismay, he said that if he had realized earlier on that is what people were out to do – make his every observation and remark public - he would have made a conscious effort to retreat into his shell.

The Einstein housekeeper stated that here employer disliked English cooking when he visited England in 1933. She says he termed their cuisine ghastly because they seemed to use mutton fat to cook all their foods. On the contrary, she says, Einstein was excited to have strawberries. She explained how much he would appreciate a strawberry dish, accompanied by whipped cream.

No Caffeine

According to Waldow, the liberal physicist, who seemed not to be bound by any religion, was not one for alcohol. Apart from celery punch–however he came up with that–he hardly touched booze. In many ways, Einstein tends to exemplify the fact that one does not need to live under stringent rules to do things that are beneficial to one's self and others. When it came to hot beverages, Einstein would drink only caffeine-free coffee and black tea. His favorite coffee was Kaffee Haag.

In Waldow's recollection, the scientist liked to watch the natural stars high in the sky, and he therefore retained a toy telescope on his desk at all times of the kind that schools have, only his was mounted on a tripod.

It is funny how some people expect scholars to be up all night studying, but Einstein, who had much more than physics to deal with went against the grain. He made it known he required a solid 10 hours of sleep in order to operate optimally.

This man who was shocked at the fat eating habits of the English was also a heavy smoker. People who were familiar with his stay at Princeton have said you would know when the good professor was walking from his house to the office just by the trail of pipe smoke he left behind.

No Socks

Einstein would never wear socks. It did not matter to him the weather, or whatever the occasion, socks were just not Einstein's thing. He would give the reason that sooner or later the socks would develop holes, so, obviously he did not see why he should have the added headache of replacing them. That habit of not wearing socks extended to the times he attended formal dinners anywhere, including the White House.

Chapter 19: Palestine and Israel

The more one knows about Einstein's life journey, the more one realizes that physics was only one of his passions. He occupied his mind, not just with thoughts of the next scientific discovery, but also of how people can live better lives.

When it came to Palestine, the land of the Arabs and Jews, Einstein philosophized about it, and also supported the people both morally and materially. He also tried to do what he could to advance peace in the region. Without question, he had clear views regarding the land and the people claiming a stake in it, most of which have been documented and secured by the Hebrew University, to which he gave so much support.

Einstein has been quoted as having said the strength of Zionism lay in its moral justification, and on that it could either stand or fail. Zionism, the movement that pushed for the establishment of a Jewish state within Palestine, had Einstein's attention, but that does not mean he concurred with every move they advocated as a means to achieve their goal. Nevertheless, he was proud of his Jewish lineage and felt the pain when he witnessed fellow Jews suffering for whatever reason.

This is easily understandable because if it hurt him to witness racial segregation in the U.S. where he was not considered to be White and was not Black, it, of course, affected him that his own people were being discriminated against.

While Einstein had listened to the argument that when Israelis fought against their neighbors, it was because they were defending themselves and what belonged to them, the Israelis, in contrast, basically did not seem to entertain the idea of that there was another group of people of Arab origin who claimed ownership to the same territory.

Equality

The conflict between the Palestinian Arabs and the Jews is complex, and it is unlikely anyone can speak of fairness without some bias. Thus far pro-Jewish hardliners have said the Arabs have no business claiming any part of the region, some moderates have said Israel should be allowed to occupy zones that they had occupied before 1967, and yet other scholars reckon 1967 is too recent to provide the Arab/Israeli borderline.

From results of past negotiations, including the Khartoum Resolution, Resolution 242, and others, as well as the response to them, it appears as if the more negotiations take place, the more confusion intensifies. This is why Einstein's option of equality might just be the plausible solution. To him, the Palestinians had as much right as the Israelis when it came to the land under conflict. His clear position was that the Jews were not superior to the Palestinian Arabs, and as such whatever solution is considered should move along a 50-50 basis.

Einstein may have skipped Bar Mitzvah lessons and the ceremony as a whole, but his argument that emphasized equal rights for the Arabs was based on morality. In fact, he categorically said that what was of paramount importance for the Jews was that they treated the Arabs among them, who happened to be the minority, as equals. He termed their ability to do that as the ultimate test of their moral standards.

He also said that it was his hope that some educated Jews, who were also spiritually alert, would lead the rest of the Jewish people to embrace the Palestinian Arabs as equals. If that happened, he averred, the Jewish people would stand a good chance of leading safe lives in a dignified manner. In an apparent episode of frustration, Einstein claimed his fellow Jewish people were, unfortunately, not sharp enough to appreciate the need for such equality, and worse still they were not intelligent enough to long for it.

Israeli Presidency

It happens to be true that the Presidency of Israel was Einstein's for the taking in 1952 when Weizmann died. The top leadership invited him to take the position because there were enough Jews who felt he deserved such honor. However, as much as no one in that community seemed to question his dignity and standing among them and in the world at large, there was still some worry among a few.

David Ben-Gurion, who was Prime Minister of Israel at the time, especially had his concerns. He was the one who had sent the official invitation to Einstein, but he disclosed to the people close to him that he did know how things would be if the revered professor actually accepted the position. Ben-Gurion appreciated the reality that Einstein's position in the Palestine situation was unique and rather radical, and without a doubt, very different from his own.

He knew if Einstein had become the president, and he remained prime minister, the country would become a leadership struggling to find common ground. One might wonder why the prime minister would proceed to invite Einstein if he believed he would have been difficult to work with, but, as he said himself, he could not afford not to invite him. In short, amongst the Jews, Einstein was like a de facto leader, and the prime minister had no choice but to acknowledge it.

At the same time, the prime minister also seemed to understand Einstein as a person because even as he invited him to take up the more or less ceremonial presidency, he secretly also hoped he would turn down the offer. As prestigious as the position was, he felt there was a good chance Einstein would refuse the offer. And it is true Einstein was interested in the welfare of the Jewish people, just as he was interested in the welfare of humanity in general. He was just not interested in big organizational or political positions.

By being interested in people's welfare, Einstein held the position that people needed to do what was required, including swallowing a bitter pill, to get things right. To the Jews, Einstein felt they needed to acknowledge that the Arabs among them had the same right as they had to live and to enjoy life in Palestine. In short, he was of the opinion that the Jews needed to accept a solution that would allow the Palestinian Arabs to own land and to build homes on an equal footing as the Jews, whether the land would be demarcated specifically for the Arabs, or not.

It was similar to what he expected from the Whites in the U.S., to accept the notion that they could sit next to Blacks in a movie theatre, or that their children could attend the same schools with the Blacks, without any harm befalling them. The idea of equality among human beings was something Einstein had been consistent with all throughout his life. He did not falter, even when the issue was close to home, as was the one of Arab-Israeli co-existence. He did wish for his people, the Jews, to have their own political state, but only by not antagonizing the Arabs in Palestine.

Israeli Hardliners

Einstein's position on Zion, Israel's headquarters, and the Arab-Israeli relationship was unpalatable to Israeli hardliners. They wanted to ignore the Arabs entirely, or at the most do them some favors, but their imagination could not stretch as far as accommodating them as equals. And yet that was the position Einstein found justifiable.

The attitude of the hardliners is evident from the coverage Einstein was given in relation to the 16th Zionist Congress that took place in 1929. The World

Zionist Organization did not mention the scientist by name and did not acknowledge him as a Zionist. Instead, in their report, he was lumped together with many other people, referred to as one among a hundred and twelve non-Zionist attendees.

When Einstein got the opportunity to address the National Labor Committee for Palestine in April 1938, he told the audience in attendance he had rather see the Palestinian Arabs and the Jews in reasonable agreement, where everyone lived in peace, than have the Jewish state established complete with geographical borders and an army. In his view, it was foolhardy to think Israel would live in peace just because it forcefully marked its territory.

Clearly, what has transpired over decades since that speech Einstein made on April 17th vindicates him. Peace for Israel and Palestinians has been elusive, and when there has been some apparent quiet, it has just been a case of undercurrents waiting to give way to angry eruptions. Einstein, though not actively religious, was aware of the tenets of the Jewish religion and the history of his people. In his argument on why he opposed the idea of a Jewish state that was exclusive of the Arabs, he cited Judaism, in addition to the practicality of such existence.

Judaism, one of the oldest monotheist religions, is very concerned about human behavior. It is generally based on The Torah, which is essentially part of the Christian Bible. The part that may have sent Einstein wondering what translations his people gave to the writings of The

Torah, was that which spelt out that the God of Judaism wished to see people do only that which is just and merciful. Keeping the Arab Palestinians out of the settlement equation was not just and merciful, as Einstein must have wondered. Some analysts have cited the deplorable living conditions of the Palestinians along the Gaza strip, the West Bank, and the refugee camps that are often established in the Middle East, to underline the importance of Einstein's position in the Arab-Israeli search for a lasting solution for peace.

In his April speech, Einstein drew the attention of the Jews to the fight they had had to endure when they did not have a state, as they strived to keep Judaism strong. Now that the creation of a Jewish state seemed imminent, he feared their actions might damage the fundamental strands and pillars that made Judaism what it was, as they agreed amongst themselves to follow narrow nationalism.

Chaim Weizmann

Fundamentalist Zionists did not want Einstein to have a say in the Israeli-Arab conflict. From as much as he had laid bare in his speeches, they clearly made for strange bedfellows. When asked a question at the beginning of 1946 on whether it was important that the Jews camping in Palestinian refugee settlements have a state of their own, his response was that he did not embrace the idea of a state. Addressing the Anglo-American Committee of Inquiry that January, Einstein said he did not see the necessity of a state in the first place, and that he linked the idea with narrow mindedness and economic limitations.

Alfred M. Lilienthal, an American Jew, who, like Einstein, was opposed to the creation of a Jewish state, said Einstein expressed similar views to him, telling him he never had been a Zionist. In his writings, Lilienthal narrates a message Einstein had sent the Jews, advising them against adopting the notion of nationalism that was being hyped. He felt if they set it aside, there would be a better chance of the Jews coexisting peacefully with the Palestinian Arabs.

Nevertheless, Einstein was aware his position represented only a minority, and was particularly unpopular among the top echelon of Jewish leadership. Lilienthal recalled Einstein, explaining to him a conversation he had had with Chaim Weizmann, and upon Einstein hearing Weizmann's side that apparently was solely on the welfare of the Jews, Einstein asked him what then would happen to the Arabs. And to Einstein's question Weizmann had retorted–What Arabs? Reportedly, Weizmann proceeded to state how inconsequential the Arabs were.

Chapter 20: Princeton

Einstein's stay in Princeton was an eventful and significant in his life. Not that his life before was without event. Before 1900, he was in Aarau, Switzerland, where he came to know the fun of romance for the first time, and where he also began to socialize like a normal teenager. Then, after his interesting life at Zurich Polytechnic, where he had enjoyed a blooming relationship with Mileva Maric, he proceeded to work in Bern.

From Bern, where he spent more than five years, Einstein had a chance to go back to Zurich to work, then on to Prague, back to Zurich, and then back to Prague again as a distinguished scholar, a member of the Prussian Academy of Science.

Einstein's happy experience in Berlin as a respected physicist, who was highly sought after, came to an end in 1932 when the Nazi Party began to gain approval in Germany. The party had capitalized on the frustration with a failing economy following the war, not because it was against the war, but because it wanted the masses to believe it could revive the economy faster. In the meantime, Einstein had relentlessly spoken against the war, and so the party that had the membership of people such as Hitler, the warmonger, did not like Einstein. By the end of 1932, Einstein's continued stay in Germany had become untenable, and he and his wife, Elsa, left for Princeton.

Princeton in Winter

Einstein was not new to it Princeton. The Ministry of Education and the Arts in Prussia had permitted him to visit the place in winter of 1930, to give lectures as a guest, for one semester. In fact, from the first time he took up the role of guest lecturer there in 1930, he made it a routine every year and thereafter would travel to Princeton in the winter season. Summer would find him in Berlin.

Einstein may have been bright and in high demand as a physicist, but he was, by no means, the first European scholar to be invited to give a lecture at an American institution of higher learning. The U.S. had gotten into the habit of inviting brilliant Europeans of high repute to visit, in a bid to have their intellectuals, and particularly scientists, learn something from them. Of course, in the years preceding WWII, it had become even more important to do so. The U.S. wanted to ensure whatever scientific knowledge and skills Europe had, the U.S. also had, and as such the country was prepared to invest in the development of science and technology.

It was with this mindset that Abraham Flexner, who had founded the U.S. Institute for Advanced Study, invited Einstein to teach at the institute when the two met at Oxford in 1931. In fact, it was along the same line that he drew a commitment from Einstein to become a regular, ensuring Einstein's financial needs while at Princeton were met and that he was not allotted fixed lecture hours. Of course, Flexner had noticed the similarity between his U.S. institution and the Kaiser Wilhelm Institutes in Germany, and he knew his institution would benefit a lot from Einstein's experience at the Berlin institutes.

As for Einstein, he, too, enjoyed meeting and exchanging ideas with other scientists, Americans included. He had particularly enjoyed the company and interesting scientific discussions he had shared with Wilson Hubble, the astronomer. The two had met at the beginning of 1931, at Mount Wilson Observatory, in California, and Einstein had been taken in by Hubble's proof of an expanding universe. In fact, that was the time Einstein stopped believing the universe was static, immediately becoming a Hubble convert.

The journey that Einstein and his wife, Elsa, took in 1932, due to the toxic environment in Germany, has already been mentioned. Suffice it to say, once in California, at the start of January 1933, the Einsteins had a stopover in Pasadena before proceeding to Princeton, this time for an indefinite stay. Back home, anti-Semitic campaigns were on the rise, and there were also waves of protest geared towards disowning Einstein and his pacifism.

Even as Einstein acknowledged, in 1932, that he was leaving Germany because of personal security concerns, he still harbored some slim hope that he might one day have a chance to make a safe return. However, he soon heard of the criminal goings on in Germany during his travel to Europe in mid-1933, while at sea aboard Belgenland, and he knew the chances of his returning were next to zero. Hence, as he travelled across mainland Europe, he wrote his resignation to the Prussian Academy.

Eventually, Einstein made the decision to become a steady resident of the U.S. and in October 1933, he, his wife, Elsa, his secretary, Helen Dukas, and his assistant, Dr. Walther Mayer, set off for the U.S, from Southampton, traveling aboard the steamship, Westernland.

Settling in at Princeton

Einstein first arrived in New York, and he was glad the atmosphere there was not too bad for him. At least, he was well received. He could not have been so certain it would be so, considering the animosity he had stirred up before as he spoke out against racial discrimination, as well as a couple of years before when he campaigned against the treatment of the Scarboro boys.

In short, it was a pleasant surprise when he and the people in his company were driven by car safely to Princeton. In the days that followed, Hans Albert, his first born son followed, and Margot, his stepdaughter, too. Maja, his sister, was later to follow the list of U.S. emigrants related to Einstein. The Einsteins were thus prepared to begin life anew.

Einstein and his family could not have settled in a better place. Not only was the place a center of excellence, it was also a place Einstein was familiar with. In fact, he had gotten to know the place in 1921, when the University of Princeton conferred upon him an honorary degree, when he also lectured on his theory of relativity. Although this time Einstein was destined to settle at the Institute for Advanced Study, he was glad for its proximity to the University of Princeton, which was at that time a renowned study center for theoretical physics, Einstein's favored discipline.

Luckily for Einstein, the institute still had a great relationship with the university, especially as they had a shared history. Although the institute was autonomous, it was initially hosted by the University of Princeton. When it was first established, its offices were within the university campus.

Professor Einstein was happy to be at an institute that focused on scientific advancement. And once there, he made it his home. Wherever he went visiting from 1933 henceforth, he would always return to Princeton. And this is where he spent the rest of his life until he died in 1955. The physical location of his office 1933–1939 was 109 Fine Hall, which today is known as Jones Hall. He would also work his experiments at the Palmer Physics Laboratory that was later converted to the Frist Campus Center.

It is clear that Einstein was in just the right place. With an institute that was well equipped to provide a great environment for research, a well-paying job, and the serenity he cherished, a community that appreciated him was just the icing on the cake. The professor of physics did not become a member of the staff at the University of Princeton; however, he would visit the place and offer his services. He would particularly help out students with challenges of a mathematical nature, and he even held a seminar on math relativity at the university.

Of course, Einstein was not the only Jewish scientist to flee Germany. There were many of them who also fled once the Nationalist Socialist Party took over power. And since a good number of them found refuge in the U.S., the tables were turned, and the mantle of scientific advancement shifted from Germany to the U.S. in the 20th century. With the pillar of physics at the Institute for Advance Study, the reputation of the institute shot up, and it became the world's most renowned research center.

Einstein enjoyed himself at the institute, particularly because of the work environment. He would spend his mornings at the institute, and then spend his afternoons at home, where he made time for friends and prominent personalities. It is worth noting that his friends and acquaintances came from different spheres, and not just science. He even socialized with people in politics. As relaxation, Einstein would go to the park and take long walks. As has been noted before, he loved nature. It can be recalled that that the time he spent time next to the lake in Berlin had been one of his most relaxing and rejuvenating.

Losing Elsa and His Best Friend

Since Einstein had made up his mind to settle in the U.S., he bought his family a house in August 1935. It was a house fit for one family and was situated along 112 Mercer Street, in Princeton. In fact, the place was very close to the institute where he worked. That house was where Elsa, Margot, and Helen Dukas lived. Sadly, barely a year after settling down at Mercer Street, Elsa fell ill. Just a couple of months later, on September 7, Einstein's dear friend, Marcel Grossman, died. Things were rapidly turning gloomy for Einstein. In December of the same year, Elsa died.

One can recall that Grossman was not just a friend. The Swiss classmate whose notes Einstein had relied on at Zurich Polytechnic was the same one who had helped him to secure a job at the patent office. And as a Mathematics professional, he had significantly helped Einstein on the math segments of his general theory of relativity. In short, Grossman occupied a special place in Einstein's heart.

Honored In Absentia

Although at Princeton Einstein was effectively in exile, it did not deter the academia from recognizing his work in science and the positive impact it had made. In 1936, Einstein was made an honorary member of the Naturforschende Gesellschaft Bern as the organization celebrated its 150th year of existence. The grand gesture took place at the University of Bern assembly hall.

Needless to say, Einstein was excited to receive the certificate of honor, and he even identified a special place for it in his flat at Princeton. There were other items he had also secured just as carefully in the house because of their sentimental value, and they included his violin, the same one he had enjoyed playing while in Switzerland and other parts of the world. It would remind him of the days when he would play Mozart or even Bach alone or with friends. Other souvenirs he took care of included his small Swiss military service book, which now lies in the archives at Jerusalem.

The Research Institute

The management and community at the Institute for Advanced Study provided a great working environment for Einstein. He did not experience any pressure and was able to do his research the best way possible. This is how he managed to advance his research to the extent of enlarging the Theory of Gravity to Unified Field Theory.

In addition to the serious scientific work he accomplished while at Princeton, Einstein was also able to advance his pacifist cause, as well as to support various Zionist organizations. For many of those passions, he was glad to have the support of his many friends and colleagues, who were particularly generous in their support for Jews emigrants.

British and American Styles

The small town of Princeton is close to Trenton, the state capital of New Jersey, and the institute where Einstein regularly worked. Princeton University has produced many notable scholars, especially in physics and mathematics, and some of them have also won the coveted Nobel Prize. Einstein enjoyed giving lectures there after settling down in Princeton.

However, the university is a private institution, with a fee that makes it somewhat exclusive, mainly accepting only students from rich families. However, the university has something in common with the Institute for Advanced Study. Besides both being centers of excellence, the architecture of their buildings, too, is almost similar. The university's buildings, close to the institute, are set within an English garden, and their architecture resembles that of Oxford and Cambridge. Both Princeton University and the Institute for Advanced Study reflect a merging of styles of both the British and the Americans.

U.S. Citizenship

Albert Einstein acquired American citizenship in October 1940. Nevertheless, he retained his Swiss citizenship that he had acquired in 1901, while in Zurich, and he still kept in touch with his friends and former colleagues in Switzerland. In 1949, in a letter he told a dear friend, Michelle Besso, who happened to be a former colleague at the Swiss patent office, that what he found best was that there still remained a few friends who were honest, and who had their head and heart just in the right place, and who also happened to understand each other as well as Einstein and Besso did.

He is also on record as having written to a friend back in Bern in a period of homesickness about how nice it had been at Kramgasse. Kramgasse is a Bern street where Einstein had rented a second floor flat.

In the early 1950s, Einstein began to experience health problems. Nevertheless, he continued working on his field theory. Unfortunately, he did not appear to be making much progress, and in the month of April 1955 he succumbed to an illness and died at the age of 76.

Einstein was well aware that he was famous, but he did not like the personality cult that often surrounded famous people. Therefore, before he died, he left instructions on how he was to be treated in death. He said he did not want a funeral service held for him, and instead, only his closest family members and very close friends could attend his cremation as a way to bid him farewell.

Patent Office in Bern

Einstein was employed at the Patent Office when he was relatively young, a little over a year of after leaving the Zurich Polytechnic. Nevertheless, it was while at that post that Einstein did so much of his groundbreaking scientific work.

Like any other graduate, he had been eager to get a job after graduating in 1900. However, since there were bad feelings between him and some influential lecturers at Zurich Polytechnic where he had studied, he could not secure an assistant's job as did the rest of his former classmates.

One great thing about Einstein was he was not one to pity himself. In this instance he instead embarked on pursuing his passion, one he did not anticipate to earn an income from, but one that would enhance his intellectual capacity, in addition to satisfying his curiosity. He began to work on his science on a serious level, even as he relentlessly applied for an assistant's job.

In February of 1901, the Swiss government granted him citizenship. Now he could go job seeking, do his academic work, pursue scientific research and everything else, on equal footing with any other Swiss national. Good things were still to follow because, in March of the same year, his inaugural scientific paper was published in Annalen der Physik, or Annals of Physics. He was now on the road to bigger things in the field of physics, and he had managed push aside the notions of Professor Weber that Einstein was not worthy of a career in science or academia.

In the meantime, Mileva Maric, Einstein's girlfriend, was at her birthplace, Hungary, and in January 1902, she gave birth to the couple's first child, a girl, named Lieserl. Einstein was very considerate because on hearing the news of the birth, he put his dissertation work on hold and used newspapers to put out offers to provide private tuition.

Beginning in May of that year to the July, he worked as a teacher at Winterthur on a temporary basis. Then, beginning in September he taught at a Schaffhausen private school. While there, he resumed his dissertation, and in November he handed it to the University of Zurich. It was in December of that year that he decided to apply for a position at the Swiss Patent Office, and Marcel Grossmann, his friend and classmate at Zurich Polytechnic, put in effort to help him get it.

Einstein felt the job in Bern would be better than doing temporary teaching jobs here and there, and so he had anxiously waited for a response from the patent office. His hopes materialized in June 1902 when he received mail from Bern with a positive response. He had applied to be considered for a job as technical expert, Class 3, within the Federal Office for Intellectual Property that was based in Bern, and that is what he got. Many referred to the office simply as the patent office. Einstein had to relocate to Bern forthwith to take up the position he had been waiting for.

Einstein's effective date of employment at the patent office was June 23, 1902. His responsibilities included assessment of the inventions presented, so as to establish if they warranted protection, if there was a chance they infringed on already existing patents, and if the inventions were really operational as stated. He earned 3,500 Swiss Francs in a year. Einstein would work diligently, leaving himself time to work on his scientific work. His efficiency and commitment earned him a salary raise, not long after being employed at the patent office. He would earn an additional 400 Swiss Francs in a year.

Olympia Academy

From the time Einstein opened up to social interactions in Aarau during his secondary school days, he never retreated back into his shell. In Bern he would meet regularly with friends who soon formed a close circle, and their main interests were physics and philosophy. They would discuss and brainstorm late into the night, all along enhancing their intellectual capacity.

The group began to refer to their close circle as the Olympia Academy. This group comprised Maurice Solovine, a Romanian student, Conrad Habicht, an old friend of Einstein's, Lucien Chavan, an electrical engineer, and Michele Angelo Besso, Einstein's great friend from his Zurich Polytechnic days.

Father's Death

Soon, a stream of happy circumstances in Einstein's life was interrupted by sadness. Einstein's father, Hermann Einstein, had a heart attack towards the end of 1902, and Einstein dashed to Milan to see him. Einstein's father had approved his son's marriage to Mileva Maric while still very ill, making it easier for Einstein's conscience, as he subsequently prepared for the wedding. Unfortunately, Hermann Einstein, died in the month of October the same year.

When his father died, it was a sad time for Einstein, who had received a lot of support from his father. However, Einstein sought to embrace life as it unfolded. In January, 1903, he married his girlfriend and mother to his daughter, although he and Maric did not have their families' blessings. Maric settled in Bern as a housewife and soon she became pregnant.

Son

Hans Albert, Einstein's first son, was born in the month of May 1904 in Bern. The couple's firstborn, Lieserl, may have been given up for adoption that autumn back in Hungary. However, besides now being happily married and a father to a lovely son, Einstein was also doing well in his scientific research.

In fact, Einstein is said to have been making wonderful progress from 1903, to 1905; arguably, the most prolific period of his career. It was in 1905 that his three major papers were published, work that ultimately transformed physics in the 20th century. The themes of the papers were Brownian motion, Special Relativity, and Quantum Theory.

Einstein's paper that dealt with Brownian motion is the one that drew the most attention to him as a scientist, attracting letters of admiration from established scientists all across Europe once it appeared in the publication, Annalen, in 1905. The paper was closely linked to Einstein's university dissertation, and it is the one that made his reputation shoot from obscurity to world prominence as an important contributor to physics. Einstein's Brownian motion was in reference to liquid particles' erratic movement that had in 1828 also drawn the attention of Robert Brown, an English botanist.

However, the paper on Brownian motion was conservative, compared to the one on light creation and transformation. The latter was drastically revolutionary, even in Einstein's own assessment, and what had driven him to formulate its related quantum hypothesis was a puzzle that existed which had bothered scientists all throughout the early 20th century. This is what Einstein was trying to respond to as he formulated Quantum Theory.

Light's Interaction with Matter

Einstein took up the challenge of advancing work on Max Planck's law, explaining it as a crucial statement in regards to the nature of light and how light interacts with matter.

Einstein was not rigid in his thinking and was quick to see logic. When it came to cause and effect, he was open to identifying the problem when he could not see logic in the classical concept. According to him, since there was the peculiar dual nature of quanta, being waves as well as particles, very likely it would be problematic to tie effects to their respective causes.

Einstein then proceeded in 1905 to illustrate that the only way light could be emitted, or even absorbed, was through discrete and finite units. The standard physical theory of the time was thus challenged by this concept, which negated the premise that light was one continuous wave. It was James Clerk Maxwell who had illustrated the movement of light as a single wave comprising electric and magnetic field back in the

1860s and 1870s, and also that atoms happened to emit light waves or absorb them in one continuous fashion. In Einstein's challenge, he showed that the waves in Maxwell's equations could only be taken as averages of the light quanta when either absorbed or emitted.

There was yet another puzzle that Einstein explained through the use of the light-quantum hypothesis he came up with, and that was the photoelectric effect. His experiment dealt with electron ejection from some metal being irradiated by light. In Einstein's experiment, he had light of varying frequencies shone on the selected metal, and once a particular frequency threshold was achieved, the metal would respond by ejecting electrons. That energy from the electrons would then rise in a curve linearly, and with the frequency of that incident light. The resultant curve happens to be independent of the brightness or intensity of that incident light.

Traditional wave theory could not explain these results because in the new scenario, the light's energy was proportional to its own intensity, in which case, energy transmitted to the electrons being ejected should match the intensity proportionately, as opposed to the frequency. In addition, the traditional view does not call for any frequency threshold in order to eject those electrons. Instead, it is expected that low frequency light, as long as it has enough brightness, should be in a position to eject electrons.

Einstein expounded the fact that if light is taken to be made up of discrete particles, which were later termed photons, each of those photons would then bear a specific amount of energy, and that is what was subsequently imparted to the electron that has been ejected. In any case, energy from a photon coming in would need to be sufficient to eject an electron, and that would, inevitably, set a frequency threshold. As such, Einstein was able to theoretically explain the energy-frequency graph, showing the photoelectric effect.

In 1905, when he introduced the idea of the photon, he suggested it was a heuristic which was helpful in explaining the photoelectric effect. He stressed that, although it is true that there are phenomena that call for particulate interpretation, there are still others that can be explained by way of wave interpretation.

In some of his papers that followed in 1906 and 1907, the great physicist was able to apply his statistical mechanics to advance the idea that light quanta exists. And henceforth, he dedicated his time to exploring the impact of the resultant wave-particle duality, which he endeavored to do by way of searching for wave unity or fusion, as well as electromagnetism particle aspects. While still at the patent office, Einstein proceeded to work on his Theory of Special Relativity.

Einstein's Footsteps

Scientists and historians have done their best to preserve the marks that Albert Einstein left wherever he went. In Switzerland, for example, where he spent his youthful years, and which is also the place where his scientific mind was at its peak, the house he lived in has been preserved. It was in Bern where, at the age of 26, he produced the most memorable works.

Einstein frequently had a group of intellectual friends around him, who were just as youthful and vibrant as he was. He also had his wife, Mileva Maric, whom he was still excited about. There was, in addition, that great working environment that the patent office provided.

Although Einstein did a lot of scientific work in Bern and also published several articles, 1905 is said to have been his best year. It was then that he published five of his key papers, leading him to refer to that year as annus mirabilis, or a miracle year. It should be remembered this was the same time he worked on and formulated his Theory of Relativity.

Einstein House

When he landed a job at the patent office, Einstein took up an upstairs two-room apartment along a famous Bern Street, No.49 Kramgasse. That is where he stayed from 1903, to 1905. The apartment was a few minutes' walk to the historic clock referred to as the Zytglogge, which was known for its hourly bell movements that would feature human and animal models.

As the energetic and ambitious Einstein walked, he would pass along the sweet shops outside that were famous for their chocolate bears, which for over 200 years had been synonymous with Bern.

Today, Bern is known for its trams and buses, and it was not much different in Einstein's days. It has historic sites that are an attraction for visitors, and the Aare River surrounds it on three of its sides. In the 1900s, Einstein would ride in tram cars on a regular basis, and it is said it was during one of those rides that he contemplated the idea of time, space, and travel and how they related to one another. It is notable that even when Einstein became famous and his career in science took him to Zurich, he still identified his stay in Bern, the City of the Bear, as the period in his life that he was happiest.

Einstein became more famous than he may have ever imagined. From childhood, his was an inclination to find out the reasoning behind happenings and situations, something that was noted early on when the magnetic compass became a real fascination for him. In his death, the world even wants to know where he walked and spent his time, the people he spoke to and what he said, and what his opinions were on various issues on science as well as outside of science.

Thus the apartment Einstein occupied when he lived in Bern has been preserved, keeping it as much as possible in a way that reflects his life of the day. In that apartment, Einstein lived with his first wife, Maric and their young son, Hans Albert. The apartment, now known as Einstein House, is considered a museum, and the public is allowed to visit.

Although Einstein was still young during his Bern days, he had traveled a lot out of necessity as he tried to build his life. He had come to Bern from Zurich, where he had trained in physics and math, and before Zurich he had lived in Aarau, still in Switzerland, as he completed the secondary school courses he had missed in Berlin. Before Aarau, he had been in Italy, where his father was running an engineering business, and, of course, these journeys had started out in Berlin where he had attended Luitpold Gymnasium. Earlier on, he had lived in Munich, Germany, with his family, although they had moved there from Ulm, still in Germany, when he was born.

Einstein, therefore, knew how to live like someone on the move. Although in Bern he was still young in his career and could not have been expected to live large, it was in his DNA anyway not to live conspicuously. His small apartment was not far from the renowned Bern Bear Pit, or Baren Graben, which is on the arcaded walkway. The actual layout of Einstein house includes a simple living room, a foyer, and anteroom. Most of the furnishings have been retained as they were when the Einsteins lived in the house. Even some family artifacts have been retained. Einstein's desk is still in the house, with a replica of his notes on display.

There are also family photographs, as well as a cradle for their young son, Hans. What surprises visitors, even as it impresses them, is that a man with such big ideas lived in humble conditions, but that did not deter him from making breakthroughs that changed the world's outlook on science.

There are still confectionary shops around that visitors enter to buy sweets as Einstein would, and it is only when they cross some bridge nearby that they get to the Bern Historic Museum at Helvetiaplatz. Close by is a permanent exhibit of Albert Einstein's Life, which was at some point a temporary display. Today, it has become the Einstein Museum.

The inception of this exhibit was 2005, when the world was celebrating a hundred years from 1905, Einstein's most significant year in terms of his work in physics. Einstein's museum is part of Bern's bigger museum, and it occupies two floors. Designers have tried to create an environment that Einstein experienced in his physicist's mind as he explored nature. Walking up the stairs, one gets a surreal feeling amidst surrounding mirrors that make people feel as if they are flying right through the cosmos. In short, the setting is an effort to reflect Einstein's imaginative mind.

Einstein Museum

Some visitors travel specifically to Bern to see the Einstein Museum; however, some want to visit it as part of their tour to the larger Bern History Museum that Einstein Museum is part of. The items and set up of the Einstein Museum reflect the scientist's life in Bern and is representative of the period that he lived, which was the start of the 20th century. The museum also shows Einstein's Jewish heritage. In addition, one gets to see the nature of his scientific work, including the theories he developed, and to gain an idea of what they mean. The museum uses different media to give visitors a good sense of Einstein. They include film documentaries and papers, audio clips and animation, and other memorabilia.

Family and Friends

In fame one is considered to be mysterious, or the public just wants to create mystery around the individual, in an attempt to explain or to justify the reason for the person being different from them. Aside from the understandable aspect of mystery, there are also some negative rumors created by those who have understandable biases and others who are jealous. Einstein, being as famous as he was, has not been spared such unfounded rumors and exaggerations. Fortunately, Einstein lived in an era when education was valued and things were documented, and so, what has been said of Einstein over the years that was untrue has been disclaimed.

The greatest physicist of the 20th century, was termed a genius, and it is possible Einstein was. Fellow scientists have particularly lauded his achievements, and the general public has admired his humility, even when his name reverberated across the world as the greatest genius ever known. What is not given much coverage, in comparison to Einstein's scientific achievements and political controversies, is his family life.

The beginning of this biography explains who Einstein's close relations were. The following section of this book reveals whether or not the world famous physicist had time to spare for his close relatives, and if they did relate with each other, what their various relationships were like.

Over the years, different correspondence has surfaced that show how he connected Einstein was to various people, including friends, and the contents usually disclose what his sentiments were towards certain individuals, including close relatives. Not fewer than 3,500 pages of Einstein's correspondence has been collected, and they give a clearer picture of the kind of character the world famous scientist was, besides being a happy recipient of the Nobel Prize.

Hanoch Gutfreund, the Albert Einstein Worldwide Exhibition's chairman, who is also associated with Jerusalem's Hebrew University, has assured the public that the recently discovered letters of Einstein's will particularly shatter the myth that Einstein was insensitive to his family.

Einstein's Letters Discovered

There has been renewed interest in the life of the intriguing physicist, Albert Einstein, and that is because some additional information about him has come to the light, and also because some aspects of his life believed to be true have been proven to be misunderstandings or outright false.

Since Einstein wrote those letters several decades ago, one may wonder why only recently they came to be known. The reason is that among the items Einstein had bequeathed to his stepdaughter, Margot, were his letters. Margot, who died in 1986, had entered into an agreement with the Hebrew University of Jerusalem in 1984, promising that she would give her stepfather's letters to the university on the condition that the university kept them sealed for 20 years after her death. Margot had appreciated how precious Einstein's letters were for posterity.

At the start of 1986, the letters had begun to reach Hebrew University, and Margot died in July of the same year. In short, the agreement between Margot, Elsa's daughter, and the Hebrew University explains why the revealing letters only surfaced in 2006. The letters are now open to viewing by the public.

Some of Einstein's letters, specifically from May to December 1920, have been published in one volume, Collected Papers of Albert Einstein, Volume 10. There is a plan to have others published as well in due course. What is currently clear is that the letters cover almost 3,500 pages, and they include letters Einstein wrote or received from his two wives and their children from 1912 to 1955.

As batches of the letters get released, the world is gaining a more vivid image of Einstein, well beyond what people knew about his personal life. The letters have been making a great impact in the way people perceived the legendary scientist, and many biographies may now need to be reviewed in the new light. It is, obviously, no one's fault that some character traits wrongly attributed to Einstein stuck for so long when the truth was so close, lying in Jerusalem. The Hebrew

University was just keeping its testament to Margot, who had inherited the letters from Einstein. It had an obligation to honor her last will to keep the letters sealed for 20 years after her death.

Surprising Truths

Some of the things fans muse at are Einstein's alleged infidelities. Could he truly have been that promiscuous, and yet his second wife, Elsa, remained loyal to him till her death? The truth that has come out from Einstein's own correspondence is that he truly was having sexual affairs with other women.

His letters to his second wife, Elsa, have disclosed a level of candidness not usual between man and wife, especially where extra-marital affairs are concerned. He had several affairs in the period beginning in the middle of the 1920s through 1933. Some affairs that have surfaced in his letters include those with a certain Margarete, Estella, Toni, and Ethel. These are women Einstein happened to spend holidays with, and even attend concerts. He would also often read books with them.

When he spoke to Elsa about it, he would try to make her understand how much women were chasing him and giving him attention he did not ask for. Much as Einstein's behavior cannot be condoned, it is easy to applaud him for acknowledging his fault, or what he termed his weakness. Professor Gutfreund explained in a letter where Einstein was consoling a son whose father had died, he told him that one of the things that made him admire the deceased was that he had lived with just one woman all through his life. He had added that for his part, he had failed immensely twice on that front. According to Gutfreund, the only consistent love Einstein had from start to the end was science.

Authorities privy to the letters reveal that the scientist communicated with Elsa and Margot in writing almost on a daily basis, whenever they were far from one another. He would talk of having delivered or listened to boring lectures, playing music with friends, or even about his efforts in trying to beat his smoking habit.

Readers are likely to find it surprising the way Einstein discussed his extra-marital affairs with his second wife and stepdaughter, and they are also likely to appreciate why his wife was so reluctant to accept these affairs. Among the love affairs Einstein had was one that involved a friend's niece, who served as his secretary. That was in 1923, and he actually did his utmost to try and integrate the young woman into his family.

Besides the women already mentioned, Einstein seemed to have had several other illicit affairs. In one of the letters to Elsa where he speaks of women hounding him, he speaks of a "Mrs. M." who was just trying to do what she enjoyed. Incidentally, Einstein, who did not show any inclination to matters of religion, chose to associate Mrs. M.'s behavior towards him with great Christian-Jewish ethics.

In the same letter, Einstein went further, highlighting the fact that Mrs. M. had not disclosed the affair to Elsa, saying it was in an effort to avoid doing something that was bound to annoy someone else, in this case, Elsa. Overall, is the weakness Einstein himself has acknowledged, that of being a womanizer. The rest of the letter appears to be an attempt to assuage the wrath, jealousy, and hurt of his wife, Elsa.

His stance is the same when he writes to Margot, Elsa's daughter, in 1931, acknowledging that Mrs. M. had followed him to England, explaining he felt her persistence to chase after him was becoming too much.

Mrs. M., a Russian Spy

A curious revelation has also surfaced about a letter Einstein had written to his Russian lover, Margarita, who is said to have been a Russian spy. In a letter to Margot, Einstein mentions a small letter he had enclosed for Margarita, to avoid curious eyes. The contents of Margarita's little letter are not known as the letter was not among those forwarded by Margot to the Hebrew university. In any case, Margot must have forwarded the letter to Margarita, as Einstein had instructed.

In June 1998, nine letters were released for auction in New York; the letters were said to have belonged to Einstein's Russian lover, Margarita Konenkova. The letters were provided by an undisclosed relative of Konenkova's. The letters that confirm Einstein's liaison with Margarita bear dates, ranging from 1945 to 1946, at the tail-end of WWII. Margarita was a married woman, but that did not seem to bother Einstein. As has been indicated elsewhere in this book, Einstein did not hold rules and restrictions in high esteem, especially when they seemed to inhibit one's natural freedom. Margarita's husband, Sergei Konenkov, was Russian as well and a sculptor. Incidentally, Margarita is also touted to have had an affair with the famous Russian pianist, Sergei Rachmaninov.

Einstein's liaison with a Russian spy might raise alarm, but it should also be remembered that Einstein was not involved with the Manhattan Project, and as such he did not have any valuable information that Margarita could have gotten from him. It is possible the Russian spy agency thought Einstein might have had access to crucial information regarding the making of nuclear weapons, having been known for his wealth of information in physics. At the same time, it is not clear when Einstein's relationship with Margarita started.

It is also not clear if Einstein began to see Margarita when Elsa was still alive, or after she had passed away. It is not just Margarita's letters from Einstein that were auctioned on June 26, but also other mementos that were part of Margarita's affair with Einstein.

Although Margarita Konenkova had little, if any, information from Einstein that could have been of use to the Russians, it has been established she actually introduced him to Soviet diplomats in the U.S. Therefore, she was clearly doing her part as a spy. As was reported in The New York Times, Paul Needham, who served as Sotheby's consultant, had stumbled on some references that were linked to Konenkova in a spymaster's book written in 1995. The author of the book, Special Tasks, is Pavel Sudoplatov and Anatoly, who are Soviet spymaster and son.

According to the book, one of Margarita Konenkova's tasks as a spy was to pay particular attention to the U.S. Manhattan Project, the secret atomic bomb-making project whose installation, Los Alamos, was within the desert of New Mexico and was headed by leading scientists, such as Robert Oppenheimer. It is clear from Special Tasks that it was Konenkova's brief to influence the U.S. scientists who mattered in the project, including Oppenheimer, many of whom she had met at Princeton University. It is worth remembering that the university was in the neighborhood of Einstein's place of residence at Princeton.

The writings have disclosed that Margarita did succeed in actually introducing Albert Einstein to the New York-based Soviet consul. And whereas it may have been upsetting for the U.S. government at the time if they had known of Einstein's liaison with a Russian spy, it is a relief to know that Einstein had no inkling of the Manhattan Project details. In short, since U.S. intelligence had denied him security clearance, there is no way he could have jeopardized the project, or even have helped the Russians with bomb-making information, either willingly, or inadvertently.

There is also nothing that may lead one to think Einstein was involved with any acts of espionage at any level. His letters, all written in German, give no reason for one to believe, or suspect, that he had any idea

Margarita, whom he met in 1935, was a spy. Margarita and her husband left the U.S. for Moscow in 1945, and records discovered in the so-called Venona Intercepts, indicate the Soviet Secret Police is entity that gave them their official papers.

This confirms that the Konenkovas were in the U.S. on a mission of espionage. The Venona project was initiated by U.S. Army Intelligence, and its main mission was to decipher intelligence messages sent by Soviet Union entities, such as the KGB, NKVD, and even the GRU.

The letters from Einstein show how close Einstein and Margarita were in the romantic sense, and not about matters affecting either the U.S., or the Soviet Union. In one of the letters, dated November 27, 1945, Einstein tells her how he had recently washed his hair on his own, and that he had not done it as well as she. He also proceeded to give her small but intimate details of his place, which he referred to as his "hermit's cell," telling her that everything there reminded him of her. In that regard, he mentioned Almar's shawl and the dictionaries, and the pipe that they had thought was gone, which he described as wonderful. Apparently, Almar stood for Albert and Margarita, a romantic elision of their two first names.

Angelo Michelle Besso

The first time Albert Einstein and Michelle Besso met was at Zurich Polytechnic as students. Besso was slightly more than five years older than Einstein, but they still made for great friends. They shared the same Jewish heritage, but Besso was a Swiss Italian. After a stint in the patent office in Bern where Marcel Grossman had helped him secure the job, he, in turn, helped his friend, Besso get on board. Both of them worked together at the patent office all the time that Einstein worked there, and they became even closer as friends.

Besso's place in Einstein's life was special. Not only did their families become friends, but Besso also provided him with much needed support as he pursued his scientific work that led to the Nobel Prize. On their way home from work, they would stroll leisurely as they discussed normal everyday events; however, soon the discussions would lead to scientific subjects.

Einstein formally appreciated and acknowledged Besso's support, and this became even clearer many years after the passing of both friends. Many people were only aware of the formal acknowledgment Einstein made when he was first recognized for his work in physics, after the four groundbreaking papers he released in 1905 brought him to the limelight. He is reported to have said his friend, Michelle Angelo Besso, had been a great collaborator in that work. What many people may not know is that there were many other instances when Einstein had expressed appreciation for Besso both with respect to his scientific pursuits and his private life.

A lot of information has come into the public domain about the relationship of the two friends, since

Christie's, a London based auction house, received Besso's letters and made them public. Christie's Head of Books & Manuscripts calls his experience when cataloguing Besso's correspondence with Einstein as "a roller coaster ride." According to him, the exercise took him through a journey that was intellectually exhilarating, endearing, and also funny.

With many people, Einstein would have spoken more generally about his work, but with Besso it is clear he was comfortable going into specifics. This was not only because he paid keen attention to Einstein's thoughts and arguments, but also because he had the intellectual capacity to comprehend. The letters Einstein sent to Besso show him discussing "special and general relativity, cosmological constant, time's arrow, red shift of spectral lines, quantum mechanics, unified theory," and other topics laid out in scientific jargon. An ordinary mind that may not understand science would still be fascinated at the level of intellectual engagement the two friends had.

Einstein's Human Side

The world may have seen and heard of the Jewish German genius with a mysteriously unique scientific mind, but Michelle Besso knew a man with the feelings of an ordinary human being, as someone who was just as concerned about his family as the next person. After all, he had had firsthand experiences with Einstein from their early 20s to their dying days, a friendship which spanned more than half a century.

In Einstein's correspondence secured at Christie's, Einstein tells Besso of the walks Einstein took with his son, then a young boy, in the mountains. He also shows his humorous side as he makes fun of his Berlin "crusty old colleagues." When discussing reactions to him on an early visit to the U.S., Einstein says he was being "shown off like a prized bull." He also discussed his experience in a meeting at the League of Nations and said he was dying of boredom. With respect to his family, he expressed anguish and feelings of remorse as his marriage to Mileva Maric broke down. In those letters, one can feel Einstein's pain as he becomes estranged with his children, Hans and Eduard.

Divorce Crucial For His Sanity

Einstein's first marriage broke down partly because of his infidelities, one of which was his romantic relationship with Elsa, who was his cousin. Besso played his role as a worthy friend in trying to keep things cool in the Einstein family, because he was particularly concerned about the couple's young sons. He would act as mediator between Einstein and Mileva. After all, the three of them went way back to their college days in Zurich.

Even Heinrich A. Medicus, a physicist, wrote in his 1994 scholarly article on Einstein of an incident where Besso and one other of Einstein's friends, Heinrich Zangger, had helped streamline things for the Einsteins after Einstein had canceled a trip to visit his family in Switzerland where he had intended to spend Christmas. Apparently, the situation between him, his wife, and sons had become a little too tense for him. Fortunately, after intervention from the two friends, Einstein reconsidered the cancelation of the trip and proceeded to join his family for the holidays.

In another of Einstein's letters to Besso Einstein expressed gratitude to him because he had been there for his wife, Mileva, and the kids. He had also explained in that July 1916 letter that the separation was for the best otherwise he would have had a mental breakdown. In fact, it was in that particular letter that Einstein converted his quantum theory into a joke as he concluded.

As serious as Einstein was in his research work, his sense of humor did not wane. This is clear from the letters he wrote to Besso, as he makes fun of himself and his fame, even about his "Jewishness" and the reality of getting old. He even found fun in his science, as evidenced in his quips about quantum physics.

There are many incidences where Einstein's vulnerable human side can be seen from his correspondence to Besso. At times he expressed his worries regarding finances, especially in relation to his son's education, and like any other human being facing day-to-day inconveniences, he would reschedule meeting plans.

There was a time when still at Princeton that he skipped years without writing to his friend, Besso, and when he wrote to him again in 1936, he attributed the omission to some "mathematical imp" stuck on his neck. The two, having been close for so many years, had a way of understanding each other. Nevertheless, analysts think the real reason Einstein had not written to Besso was his attention to Elsa, whose health had been on a progressive, painful decline. She had been suffering from heart and kidney ailments and died that same year.

When Einstein lost his wife, Elsa, and WWI came, he seemed to stop communicating with friends for a while, probably because circumstances were not conducive, or because he wanted to shield himself from the outside. He found refuge in his work, spending long hours at it. In a letter Einstein sent to Besso from Princeton on July 10, 1938, he told him life would not have had meaning if he did not have his work.

It is thought Einstein may have begun a romantic relationship with Margarita Konenkova by the time he wrote the letter to Besso. Although all information indicates Einstein was in the dark about Margarita's link to Russia's spy agency, the woman who is said to have been romantically involved with other influential men, such as music composer, Rachmaninoff already had a spy code. In the spy circles, they referred to her as Lukas.

As Einstein and Besso advanced in age and kept in touch, Einstein's letters seemed to reflect not only a philosophical attitude towards issues, but also a spiritual feel. As he spoke of taking delight at his work and relishing development of a new theory, he reflected a feeling of elevation to a level where he could grasp fundamental truths. In one of his letters, he expressed such feelings as "getting closer to God."

Chapter 21: Hans Albert

Hans Albert was Einstein's son with Mileva Maric, the Hungarian Serb he met at Zurich Polytechnic. Hans was born on May 14, 1904 after his parents had married, and when they were both living in Bern, Switzerland. He never got to meet his sister, who had been born before him, because her mother did not bring her to Bern when she left Hungary to come join her then boyfriend, Einstein, and because the family as a whole lost touch with her forthwith.

At the time, his father was working at the Swiss patent office, and he related with his son the normal way a father does. To Albert Einstein's credit, while this was a period when he had a lot going on his research front, he still made time to be with Hans, and to take care of him. Mileva once wrote that her husband spent most of his leisure time at home, usually engaging his son in play.

As aforementioned, many often find solace in creating rumors and myths surrounding celebrities when they are not close enough to learn about their lives firsthand. This also happened with Einstein, and unfortunately, some of the rumors portray him as a man who was obsessed with his scientific achievements at the expense of his children. This is not the case, as various authentic documents emerging reveal a normal loving father.

It is important to note that even as Einstein's health deteriorated, his son, Hans Albert, spent a significant amount of time at his father's bedside in Princeton. It is also important to note that Einstein took care of Hans

Albert's education, until he built a career of his own choice. Unlike his father who was German by birth, Hans was Swiss. He was not only born in Switzerland, but his birth was at a time when his father had taken up Swiss citizenship.

Hans' Adolescence and Teen Years

Once Einstein and Mileva parted ways, Einstein lost the opportunity to be with his sons on a full-time basis, or even on a regular basis. As he wrote to his friend, Zangger, it pained him, but he could not bear to continue being married to Mileva.

As such, Hans was under the care of his mother through adolescence and teenage years. Hans grew to become a decent, independent man in his youth, manifesting a high level of intelligence. Gladly, for both father and son, Einstein was able to pay visits to the family in Zurich where they lived. Einstein would also write loving letters to his son, and plan for expeditions that they would go on together when it was convenient for them both.

Of course, it was not always smooth sailing, as can be seen in a letter Einstein wrote to his friend, Zangger. There were times Einstein sensed some form of tension, especially when Hans failed to respond to his letters as fast as was normal for him, and he attributed it to negative influence from the mother.

Nevertheless, father and son managed to relate well, and his father was proud that he was doing well academically. Hans passed his A-levels and proceeded to pursue engineering. As already mentioned, he began with his parents' old college, ETH, in Zurich. Hans ended up becoming a civil engineer and graduated in 1926. Although he climbed up the career ladder to become a professor of Hydraulic Engineering and generally a renowned engineer in the US, he began low just as his father. His first job was in Dortmund as a designer in the field of steel construction.

Hans Albert must have admired the route his father had taken in his academic pursuits, because he, too, went to Zurich Polytechnic, or the Swiss Federal Institute of Technology (ETH), when it was time for higher education. While his father had received a diploma in teaching physics and mathematics in 1900, Hans received a civil engineering diploma in 1926. For around four years, until 1930, Hans worked as a steel designer in Dortmund on a bridge project. Then in 1936 he received a doctorate in technical science.

Hans' Finances

Engelbert Schücking, son of Lothar Engelbert Schücking, who was a lawyer in Dortmund, and who lived from 1873 to 1943, inherited a postcard from his father. The card explains a situation where Hans Albert, who was then an engineer in the same city of Dortmund, made legal consultations with the older Schücking, but he had difficulties settling the bill. The two, nevertheless, agreed to have Hans bring a piece of document autographed by his father, Einstein, who had by then become very famous.

Schücking was in possession of a postcard written by his father, dated Jan 24, 1929, to prompt Hans Albert, regarding the promise of an autographed document. His father had clearly spelt out to Hans that he wanted written by Einstein in his own hand. It was obvious from the letter Lothar Schücking wrote to Hans Albert that Schücking had an autograph collection.

In a response on March 11, Hans Albert had explained the challenges that had caused the delay in fulfilling his promise, and one of them was that when it came to such matters as writing autographs, his father was peculiar. The authentic documents from Schücking show that Albert Einstein had not refused to give his son an autograph. They also do not give any notion there having been bad blood between father and son. Hans had attributed the delay to his father's nature in general, meaning that Hans may have had to do a little coaxing, or just be patient with the old man.

In that same response, Hans Albert had explained that he had suffered influenza, and there had also been a death in the family. In addition, he had taken time to relocate. In short, there was a set of challenges delaying the process of Albert getting an autographed document from his father, and not just Einstein's outlook on such things. When Schücking was writing the postcard, Einstein was at the peak of his fame. In fact, only three days before, his six-page paper on the unification of gravity and electromagnetism had just been published by the Prussian Academy of Sciences.

Hans Grown Up

In a postcard that Einstein sent to his son, Hans Albert, in Feb 1929, he expresses joy that his son was enjoying his profession. He spoke of piano transport expenses, telling his son to let him know how much it had cost to transport the piano, so that Einstein could reimburse him. He explained how much he liked the piano and how difficult it was to find a good one at a reasonable price.

Albert Einstein then asked Hans to pass his condolences to his wife, Frieda. Apparently she had some misfortune. He proceeded to inform Hans of their plans to buy a small size summer house within Ferch, next to Berlin, saying the sailing would be lovely. He told Hans in that regard that the place would be good for him and his wife, Frieda. In a light tone, he had told his son in the letter that they wished to live like gypsies in that summer house, starting the coming May to September.

Of course, Einstein and Elsa never got to buy the summer house they had intended to secure south-west of Potsdam, Berlin, because the city offered Einstein one as his 50th birthday present. And although they spent the summer there, the mayor's offer to have Einstein taking possession of the house for good did not materialize due to bureaucratic red tape. That was when Einstein gave up on the summer house and proceeded to build a home in Caputh, which is in close proximity to Ferch.

Albert Einstein had signed the postcard just as he did his letters, but this time he made a point of telling his son he could pass on the card as an autograph. This goes to show that Albert Einstein and his son, Hans, were on good terms and shared correspondence and events as is the case in a normal father-son relationship.

The reason many people tend to think the two did not see eye to eye was perhaps because their relationship had been a little strained when Han's mother, Mileva, separated from Einstein. Hans hence had an absentee father, and since he had been used to having him around, the separation must have hit him hard. Understandably, too, he must have sympathized with his mother, who was doing her best to care for him and his brother, Eduard.

To make a strained relationship worse, Hans Albert got involved with a woman who was much older than he was, and his father did not like it. He actually spoke openly against it, and when his son was adamant he was going to marry her, his father told him not to hesitate to approach him for advice if ever he felt he wanted to file for divorce. As far as the elder Einstein was concerned, Han's marriage to Frieda was doomed to fail. Obviously, it did not fail, and father and son soon began to get along.

To a keen observer, the situation must have looked like a case of what goes around actually coming around, because Albert Einstein's parents themselves had not been supportive of Einstein's marriage to Mileva Maric in the beginning.

Part of father-son relationship mending properly was probably a result of Hans Albert getting to understand that there were some marriages that failed to work, even when there was no bad blood between the partners. That was likely why father and son were fine by the time Hans himself established a family. In any case, Einstein had ensured that his children did not lack in school fees and other provisions, and Hans was bright enough to know that.

Adolescent Son

Einstein's letters that have been made public have actually cleared Einstein's social image to a great extent. He was in constant communication with his children as they grew up, even if he did not live with their mother, yet the image the world got from hearsay was not pleasant. Some portrayed him as a reckless father, probably because he was unable to hold his first marriage intact and also because he had acknowledged womanizing. Nevertheless, the fact of being a poor husband did not make him necessarily, even practically, a poor father. The letters have shown he was a caring and loving father.

In addition to those already discussed in this book, there was one he wrote to Hans Albert when he was only 11, and in it the reader senses the strong feelings of a loving father. The letter opens by Einstein confirming receipt of his son's letter, and declaring joy at receiving it. He then proceeds to express his fears, saying he had been afraid his son would not continue writing him.

He then openly broaches another subject, reminding Hans he had told him while in Zurich that it was awkward for him whenever Einstein went there. He therefore suggests they meet in a different location where no one would interfere with their comfort. Einstein then expressed his wish that he and his son be spending at least one month together every year, so that Hans can see that he truly has a father who loves him and is fond of him.

In that same letter, Einstein tells Hans there are several good and beautiful things he could learn from him, things that he could not easily get from another person. He tells him there were many things he had acquired through a lot of strain that would benefit strangers, and that his sons, more so, should be able to benefit from them. Einstein even mentions his work's progress to his son in that letter, telling him he had just accomplished an important part of his work, which he would explain to him when he was older.

Einstein then speaks of the piano, expressing happiness that Hans was enjoying playing it. He gives him his opinion that playing the piano and carpentry are the best pursuits for his age, saying they are better than even school. On the piano specifically, Einstein advises his son to concentrate on things that please him, and that even if his teacher did not focus on them, it would be good if Hans focuses on them. Einstein tells his son that was the best way to learn, engaging in something with such great enjoyment that one does not realize time passing. He then tells him that he was speaking out of experience, saying he was sometimes wrapped up in his work in a way that even made him forget lunch.

Einstein ends that 1915 letter by asking Hans to kiss his kid brother, Tete, on behalf of his dad. Tete was the family nickname for Eduard. There is no way a father who did not care for his children could write such a letter. It should also be noted that these are authentic letters that were handed over from people who inherited them from the source.

In the U.S.

When Hans Albert and his family came to live in Greenville, South Carolina, in 1938, it was in response to his father's advice, who had asked him to leave Switzerland and relocate to the US. Hans had worked in the country's department of Agriculture (USDA) as he studied sediment transport, and his course study took from 1938, to 1943.

After graduating, he still continued to work for the USDA and was based at the California Institute of Technology from 1943. He became an Associate Professor of Hydraulic Engineering, at University of California, Berkeley, later advancing to a full professor, and subsequently professor emeritus. His career took him to different parts of the world, where conferences in hydraulic engineering conferences were held, just as his father, Albert Einstein, had traveled to participate in physics-related conferences. From Hans' career success, it is safe to say he was truly his father's son.

Chapter 22: Fellow Scientists

As aforementioned, Einstein came to Princeton the first time in 1921 to give a lecture, the same occasion the university honored him with a degree. What is yet to be clarified is that his presentation was part of the university's Stafford Little Lectures, and his was on the Theory of Relativity. He ended up giving five lectures during that visit. And when he next returned to Princeton in 1933, it would turn out to be a 22-year long stay till death took him in 1955.

The first time he was at the university, during a two month visit, it was a matter of going with the flow because initially he had set out for the U.S. to help out the Zionist movement advance its cause. Nevertheless, he ended up receiving an invitation by the University of Princeton, and the rest is history. The reason he felt compelled to give a series of science-related lectures at the university at the time was that the university had invested a lot of time working with the Theory of Relativity, in comparison to other U.S. institutions.

During the ceremony to confer him an honorary degree, which was held in Alexander Hall, Einstein had been welcomed by President Hibben, who spoke in German. Dean Andrew Fleming West then proceeded to read his citation, in which he saluted him as the Columbus of science, who had voyaged through unknown seas all alone. Hall finally conferred to him Princeton's honorary degree of Doctor of Science.

Stafford Little Lectures

When Einstein, in his heyday, gave his five Stafford Little Lectures, the university's famous McCosh Hall was packed with scientists from all over the globe. Einstein had given his lectures in German, and Edwin P. Adams, a fellow physicist from the university had provided a précis of each of them in English.

According to the Daily Princetonian, Adams was in the group of leading U.S. expositors of Einstein's Theory of Telativity. Others like Adam included Princeton's Luther P. Eisenhart, a mathematician, and Henry Norris Russell, an astrophysicist, also from the University of Princeton.

The lectures at Princeton were so successful and so valued that their transcripts were polished and presented to Einstein to revise and approve, and then Professor Adams translated them into English to be published by the Princeton University Press. The university press then distinguished itself as the first U.S. publisher to produce a book by the world's most revered scientist of the day and the century. The publication was titled, The Meaning of Relativity, and it has been republished no fewer than five times and is still being printed.

Once Einstein accepted the job at Princeton's institute, he made Princeton his home without reservations. Many of the members who comprised the faculty at the institute had formerly been members of staff at the university. Einstein remained at the university campus location until construction of the institute's first building was completed in 1939, occupying Room 109.

His four other colleagues were settled at the university's former Fine Hall. That building has always held tributes that are in praise to Einstein's genius. It has equations of relativity, among other motifs, all laid out on the leaded windows. And just over the Common Room's fireplace, there is one famous remark of his that declares "God is not malicious at all, although He is subtle."

Albert Einstein continued to grow and develop with the institute. From his office within the mathematics building at the university, to Room 109 at the institute, and next to the ground floor of Fuld Hall of the institute, for which construction was accomplished in 1939. His daily routine became a mile and a half walk from his house on 112 Mercer Street, to Fuld Hall. In explaining to friends and relatives how he had settled down, he termed the Princeton quiet life as "indescribably enjoyable." To Max Born, his fellow physicist friend, he used the term "splendidly" when explaining how he had settled down.

Einstein would work nicely in the serenity of the institute and his house, the reason he went further to use the analogy of a bear hibernating in its cave when telling Max about the kind of life he led at Princeton. He told him he had never before experienced the homeliness he felt at Princeton. For leisure, the violin had its place in Einstein's life as it had in the other places he had lived. He and friends would hold musical evenings, and on some days sail on Lake Carnegie in a small secondhand boat. He would also enjoy walks in the countryside bordering the institute.

Relativity's 3rd, 4th and 5th Editions Printed by Princeton Press

Einstein's respect never faded with age or familiarity. At Princeton, the academic community and everyone else held him in high esteem. He continued working on the theme of general relativity as well as the interpretation of the Quantum Theory. He also had work on the Unified Field Theory on his table. Still at Princeton, but after WWII, he became actively involved in the discussion on nuclear control as well as world peace, and he used his prominence to advocate peace on the world stage.

On Einstein's 70th birthday, he was humbled to have around 300 scientists celebrate with him. They gathered at the Frick Chemical Laboratory where a symposium was held, highlighting the contributions he had made to modern science. The symposium was held under the collaboration of the University of Princeton and the Institute of Advanced Study. On that occasion, J. Robert Oppenheimer, the institute's director, expressed the high esteem with which the universal fraternity of scientists held Einstein. To underline the sentiments, Oppenheimer referred to Einstein as their brotherhood's greatest member.

The Greatest

Even in death, the fraternity of scientists still held Einstein in extremely high regard. On learning of his death, the Daily Princetonian had an entire issue dedicated to him. In it were tributes sent by friends and colleagues. Einstein's neighbor at Mercer Street and Chair of the Department of Physics, Allen G.Shenstone, referred to him as the most beautiful character ever known to him. Einstein's humility was also not forgotten.

The University Research Board chairman, Henry D. Smyth, who was also Atomic Energy Commission's former member, highlighted the informality, as well as simplicity with which Einstein related with scientists of lower cadres and ages. He also added that the field of physics and Princeton as a whole had benefitted in immeasurable ways from Einstein's presence at the Princeton institute.

The Institute of Advanced Study issued a statement voicing the sentiments of Einstein's colleagues, which were taken to be the general feeling of everyone across the globe. The general sentiments were that Professor Albert Einstein was among mankind's greatest personalities, who had struggled for intellectual insight and general improvement of morals. It also carried the general belief that Einstein had secured himself some high ground in the annals of history.

Einstein's Memory

Ever since Einstein died in 1955, Princeton has made a point of keeping his memory alive. For example, in 1966, the University of Princeton, in league with the Institute of Advanced Study sponsored the production of a U.S. postage stamp that bore his photograph, courtesy of Philippe Halsman, which was issued in Princeton. That issue coincided with Einstein's 87th birthday anniversary.

Then, in 1975, the International Business Machines (IBM) Corporation gave the University of Princeton a grant of one million dollars as a university professorship in Einstein's name. The first scholar to benefit from the grant was Robert H. Dicke, who at some point had been Chairman of the Department of Physics at the institution. Dicke was recognized for his field of gravity studies and also for crucial experimental tests he had conducted on Einstein's famed General Theory of Relativity. Thus, Dicke took up the title of Albert Einstein Professor of Science.

Within the same period of mid-1970s, there were plans by the Princeton University Press to publish Einstein's papers; the idea was to run in excess of 20 volumes. When that plan was in the pipeline, The New York Times reported the project as being among the most ambitious venture of the century by a publishing firm.

Chapter 23: Support System

Albert Einstein did not try to reinvent the wheels sought to explain phenomena that other people had taken for granted or had not noticed. At the end of the day, the theories he created from his analysis changed various scientific views and became the basis for other serious scientific work. However, the great physicist did not climb the ladder of success single-handedly. He, in fact, had an inconspicuous support system.

When support is mentioned, one usually thinks of those such as Einstein's father, who gave him a magnet that piqued the young Einstein's curiosity, and who sponsored him to Zurich Polytechnic, despite the son having abandoned the Luitpold Gymnasium prematurely. One also thinks of his uncle, who had given him books to read on his own. However, there are others who helped Einstein accomplish his serious work.

Climb to Success

When, in November 1915, the Prussian Academy of Sciences published Albert Einstein's General Theory of Relativity in a series of four short papers, the physicist's fame reverberated beyond Berlin and reached the world stage. Fellow scientists termed him a genius, for they could comprehend the keenness, high-level analysis, and intensity of work that must have been involved for such an accomplishment. What the world hardly knew were the people working with him either directly, or indirectly.

The fact that Einstein had a strong support system should not be surprising, really, because even a good surgeon can only work well with a team of support staff, and great athletes need people to cheer them on. In short, the genius had people in his life who warrant some acclaim, too. Some are fellow scientists, while others did not pursue their science careers to very significant levels.

Einstein received the professional tools of trade he required to pursue his science career at Swiss Federal Polytechnic, simply referred to in this book as Zurich Polytechnic, although he supplemented his formal learning with his own reading. The institution was later renamed the Swiss Federal Institute of Technology (Eidgenössische Technische Hochschule or simply ETH.

Besso, Grossman, and Einstein's Father

During Einstein's stay in Zurich, he met Marcel Grossman and Michele Besso, who ended up becoming great personal friends of his. They were all young men at the time and had a lot of enthusiasm for whatever they did. Of course, this was the institution that gave the three friends their real career foundations. Just to recap, Einstein's stay at the college studying physics and mathematics began in 1896 and ended in 1900. The beginning of Grossman's support for Einstein has already been noted, as it was his class notes Einstein relied upon for his revision as he had been often skipping classes.

Grossman's great talent was in mathematics, and whenever Einstein's work had a mathematical angle, Grossman was his go-to person. He was also well organized and would help Einstein streamline his work, as opposed to taking too long in the fanciful phase. As for Besso, he was an engineer with a highly imaginative mind, only he was a little disorganized. He was not only available when Einstein wanted someone with whom to brainstorm, but he was also Einstein's rock in his social life, to the extent of bringing sanity to his home when there was a storm raging.

Although books often speak of Grossman and Einstein, it is important to note that Marcel, the young man, did not have enough clout to get Einstein a job when he was rejected as an assistant at the Polytechnic. The force behind Einstein's recruitment at the Patent Office was Marcel Grossman's father, a businessman, who ensured his son's friend was employed by 1902. And it is already known, the patent office is the place that offered Einstein the environment conducive to producing the scientific papers that he published early in life.

Besso who joined Einstein later in Bern was Einstein's daily audience as he thought out his ideas aloud and even as he tried to work out his scientific problems from different angles. With a good science background and a highly imaginative mind, Besso was a great help to Einstein. Without him, probably Einstein would have been stuck in some phases too long, or even gotten too frustrated to continue. In fact, it is telling that Einstein could not resist acknowledging Besso's support in his famous papers published in 1905, the same year he completed his dissertation, leading to his Ph.D. in Physics.

Conrad Habicht

Members of the self-declared Olympia Academy were also helpful in keeping Einstein's mind alert. In 1907, he wrote to one of his friends from that group, Conrad Habicht, when he began contemplating extending the relativity principle from uniform motion to an arbitrary one through a theory of gravity. He explained to Habicht what he hoped his new theory would achieve and what scientific discrepancies it would account for. Of course, Einstein could not have explained such things to Habicht unless he thought his input was important.

Research work being a process, not only involving personal study, but also evaluation and incorporation of feedback, Einstein's took years. He did not complete the work he had begun on the new theory while at the patent office in Bern. He was only able to dig significantly deeper into it when he joined the University of Zurich in 1909 as a professor. As he studied, researched, and consulted, Einstein expanded his comprehension of his project. He was still upbeat when he moved to Charles University in Prague two years later, and soon he came to the realization that it was necessary to incorporate gravity into the space-time structure he had been working on.

When he reunited with Marcel Grossman at Zurich in 1912, the two combined forces to generate a complete theory, relying primarily on the Gauss' curved surfaces theory. Of course, it is likely Einstein learned of this theory from Grossman, his great go-to mathematician. What is not in doubt, because it is documented, is that Einstein had told Grossman he had to help him otherwise he would go nuts. The collaboration they had, which resulted in a joint publication in June 1913, has been highlighted in the scientist's Zurich notebook. The joint work was titled, Entwurf ('outline') paper.

This was, essentially, the work Einstein advanced upon to build the general theory of relativity. While his joint paper with Grossman was severely limited in how the covariance equations worked, the ones in the General Relativity Theory that Einstein developed were solid. A lot of high level thinking was, definitely, involved in coming up with field equations that retained their form whatever coordinates were used in their expression, but the bottom line is that Einstein did not have to go back to Square One. He had the framework to work with, which he and his colleague and friend, Grossman, had built.

Kottler and Others

Serious work of an earth-shaking magnitude, such as Einstein's was usually has pillars to sustain it, or a reliable foundation upon which it sits. Einstein's General Theory of Relativity sat on the foundation of the Entwurf theory, but even Einstein and Grossman had relied on other scientist's work when developing this theory. Thus, the chain of people who contributed to Einstein's success, albeit indirectly, becomes longer.

First there was the energy-momentum tensor, for which its inaugural appearance was in 1907/8, when the Electrodynamics Theory of James Clerk Maxwell and Hendrik Antoon Lorentz was reformulated in special relativity by Hermann Minkowski. That was when it dawned on scientists that it was possible to define energy-momentum tensor for physical systems, and not just for electromagnetic fields.

When in 1911 Max Laue released his book, Das Relativitätsprinzip, which was on special relativity, the tensor had taken center stage in the renewed relativistic mechanics. The following year Friedrich Kottler, a youthful Viennese physicist, took Laue's formalism and generalized it from flat space-time, to curved space-time. That is the generalization that the Einstein-Grossman duo relied upon to formulate their Entwurf theory. The importance of the people whose great scientific work preceded Einstein's is reaffirmed by the fact that Einstein publicly acknowledged Kottler during a lecture in Vienna, asking him to stand up to be recognized for his work.

Reverting to Michele Besso again, Einstein worked with him in the summer of 1912, carrying out further investigations on the Entwurf theory, whose calculations are well-preserved within the Einstein-Besso 1913 manuscript. For Besso, it was not just the calculations he did. He also raised pertinent thought-provoking questions. Some of them got Einstein thinking about the Entwurf field equations in relation to the gravitational field of the sun. Some of the scientific arguments that Einstein came up with later were result of those interesting questions that Besso raised as they worked.

Among the aspects of the Entwurf equations Einstein and Besso checked was if the equations held where a rotating coordinate system was concerned. They were concerned about the inertia rotation forces, such as the centrifugal force experienced while on a merry-go-round, and that force appeared to pass the test of being of a gravitational nature. However, Besso was not satisfied and warned Einstein the centrifugal force was in reality not a gravitational force. Einstein ignored Besso's warning, but Besso was later vindicated.

Einstein and Grossmann made their final touches of their joint Entwurf paper around May 1913, the same time Einstein was invited to give a lecture before the Society of German Natural Scientists and Physicians scheduled for September. The meeting of great scientific minds was to be held in Vienna. That invitation for a 34 year old scientist was testament to the high esteem with which Einstein was held by his fellow scientists. It was also an affirmation to Einstein that he was on the right track.

A couple of months after the invitation, in July 1913, some renowned physicists, Max Planck and Walther Nernst, came knocking. They wanted to uproot Einstein from Zurich on a generous offer, to go join their Prussian Academy of Sciences, which was based in Berlin. Their offer had a big pay package and a teaching-free position. Einstein knew what the offer meant in terms of being able to advance his scientific work, and he therefore accepted the job without hesitation. His new engagement officially commenced in March 1914.

These two scientists who happened to be senior at the academy they had inducted Einstein into were interested in Einstein's contribution to quantum physics and were less interested in the work he had been doing on gravity. Many theories relating to gravity had been proposed, including one that had been formulated by Gunnar Nordström, a youthful Finnish physicist. Einstein incorporated Nordström's theory in his Vienna lecture together with the Entwurf theory he and Grossman had formulated, after working on both from May to August 1913.

Nordström then visited Einstein in Zurich during the summer of 1913, and they had a discussion regarding both of their theories. Einstein was trying to explain to Nordström how the gravitational field source in the two theories needed to be constructed, the representation of the density and flow of energy and momentum, and such other aspects of their theories.

Later, in September, when he gave his lecture before fellow scientists in Vienna, Einstein concluded that there was need for more experiments to be conducted on both the Entwurf theory and that of Nordström. Erwin Finlay Freundlich, a low level astronomer from Berlin, with whom Einstein had kept in touch with since his Prague days, was set to establish if Einstein's theory worked. He set out for Crimea in August 1914, purposely to watch the solar eclipse. He wished to determine if gravity really does bend light. Unfortunately, it was the time when WWI was breaking out, and he was held up by the Russians. In short, Freundlish's mission was aborted.

While in Zurich, Einstein had the precious opportunity to work with Adriaan Fokker, a youthful physicist and Lorentz student, and both of them tried to rework the Nordström theory. What Einstein did was to introduce the same form of mathematics the Entwurf theory was based on, and it was then that they were able to see that in both the Nordström and his theory with Grossman it was possible to incorporate the gravitational field into the curved space-time structure. The two comparisons gave Einstein a more vivid picture of the Entwurf theory structure, which enabled him and Grossman to work on another paper on that theory as a joint effort. That second paper was published in May 1914, but Einstein was already at the academy in Berlin.

Astronomer, Arthur Eddington

In Einstein's successes of the period, therefore, a physicist like Fokker warrants a mention, and Grossman's place is even more important. As for the Entwurf theory that Freundlish could not test due to the outbreak of WWI, it took a whole five years for it to be proven, this time by Arthur Eddington, English astronomer.

In 1919, Eddington watched another eclipse and noted how the distant stars were deflected when seen in close proximity to the edge of the Sun. In that incident, he confirmed that the light bent just as Einstein had predicted. That was the moment that made Albert Einstein more than a lecturer of physics, making him a household name. Clearly, if Eddington had not cared to test Einstein's theory, and if Einstein had not collaborated with Grossman to begin building it, this monumental achievement by Einstein either may not have come to pass, or it may have been delayed.

Questioning Einstein's Premise

Michelle Angelo Besso, Einstein's buddy in science and close private confidante, had earlier questioned Einstein's premise that centrifugal and gravitational force was essentially the same. Now the time had come when Einstein had no choice but to admit that Besso had been right. At the Prussian Academy of Sciences, people were not interested in his gravity-related theory, so he had shoved aside. However, he came to notice that the theory–the Entwurf Theory–seemed to interest physicists in other parts of the world, such as Paul Ehrenfest and Lorentz from Leiden in Netherlands.

By this time Einstein had parted with his first wife, Mileva Maric, and she had gone to live in Zurich and taken the children with her. Einstein, renewed the affair with his cousin, Elsa, and feeling confident enough to resume serious research, began to write an exposition of the Entwurf theory. That was towards end of 1914. However, he realized after giving a number of lectures in Göttingen that David Hilbert, the renowned mathematician, had become very interested in

Einstein's work. Einstein became a little uneasy and decided to review his work.

To his utter dismay, he found out that Besso's warning had been timely. The Entwurf theory did not at all make rotational motion relative. Einstein wrote to seek the help of Freundlich, telling him unfortunately his mind happened to be in a rut, but the astronomer was not able to help. The jocular Einstein had written in the letter to Freundlich that he hoped the young man's brain matter that was not yet spoilt could identify where errors were emerging from.

Clearly, not only were people offering help. Einstein himself was going out to seek it when he was stuck. This time he had an emergency, as he feared the great mathematician would beat him in establishing the deficiencies of his theory. His mind went into overdrive, and soon, he identified the field equations as the weak link. In the early days of November 1915, he quickly came up with fresh equations and got them printed, although he was not so sure they were his final. A week later, he reviewed those field equations, replacing them with others. And he made another review two weeks later in papers that he submitted to the Prussian Academy, confident that this time round, the Entwurf theory field equations were, on the overall, covariant.

When Einstein wrote his first paper in November, he admitted the theory was a great triumph that exalted Carl Friedrich Gauss' and Bernhard Riemann's mathematics. He noted how he and his colleague, Grossman, had initially considered the equations he had finally come to and then dismissed them. He suggested they would have gotten it right the first time if only they had allowed pure mathematics to guide them, as opposed to leaning too much towards physics. Here, Einstein was again affirming without the knowledge of his readers that if only he had heeded Besso's warning, he would not have proceeded to publish a theory in which the equations were of limited covariance.

Chapter 24: Medical Friends

Talmey, Ophthalmologist

Max Talmey and Albert Einstein became friends when Einstein was in his adolescence. Talmey was Polish and 10 years older than Einstein. He had come to Munich to pursue studies at the Munich medical school, and he would lend young Einstein books on science and technology, and even some on mathematics and philosophy. That must have helped piqued Einstein's interest in science even further.

For the time that Einstein's family lived in Munich, they had, as was normal with families, a family physician. Talmey happened to be a brother to the family doctor who attended to the Einsteins, and he got to know them and associated with them for the five years he lived in Berlin, Germany. Before that, he had lived in Russia. Talmey became a family friend to the Einstein's, and he would join them once a week for dinner. As the friendship between him and the Einstein's solidified, he became a mentor to young Einstein, whom he watched grow from a 10 year old boy to a 15 year old before he left Berlin.

Some of the books Talmey introduced Einstein to early in life included Naturwissenschaftliche Volksbiicher, by Aaron Bernstein and Kraft und Stoff, by Ludwig Btichner. Apparently, Bernstein had a number of books on natural science that laymen were interested in. Nevertheless, the book that got Einstein particularly interested in physics was Btichner's Kraft und Stoff, which tackled force and matter. The author is seen to have gathered scientific knowledge that prevailed in those days, and organized it to form a kind of philosophical concept of the universe. In short, Max Talmey can be aptly credited with introducing Einstein into the real scientific world.

Max Talmey was born in 1869, graduated from Munich University in 1889, and finally landed in the U.S. at the onset of the 20th century where he continued practicing medicine. He died in 1941, but not before authoring a book on physics, The Relativity Theory Simplified, and the Formative Years of the Inventor, published in 1932.

When Talmey immigrated to the U.S., he continued his career in medicine, but he mainly practiced ophthalmology in the city of New York. The field of medicine has benefited significantly from his contributions, but like Einstein, he had a broad mind. He contributed immensely as well to the promotion of international languages, and also played a big role in promoting the works of Einstein.

Although the two friends took a break from communicating when they both left Berlin, they rekindled that closeness when Einstein visited the U.S. the first time, and the friendship grew as he relocated to the U.S. for good.

Zangger, Forensic Pathologist

Albert Einstein and Heinrich Zangger met in Zurich and struck up a friendship. Zangger was just a little older than Einstein, having been born in 1874. During Einstein's stay in Zurich, Zangger was the Director at the Institute of Forensic Medicine, which was part of the University of Zurich.

Their first meeting was in 1905, and the point of their discussion was Brownian motion. Soon, Zangger became Einstein's confidante, not only professionally, but also in matters of a personal nature. In fact, he was instrumental in having Einstein leave Prague and return to Zurich in 1913.

Einstein kept in touch with Zangger and corresponded through letters whenever he was out of Zurich. Their bond was so tight that Zangger became a father figure to Einstein's children, after the separation of Einstein and Mileva Maric in 1914. Einstein would also write to Zangger seeking advice on varied serious issues involving his life, and other times, he would write just to ventilate.

For instance, just a day after Einstein submitted the General Theory of Relativity's final version to the Royal Prussian Academy of Sciences, he wrote to Zangger, and in the letter he expressed his sentiments on a wide range of issues. That letter, one among Einstein's letters that have been made public, was dated November 26, 1915.

First, Einstein was excited about his work on the theory, terming the theory one of "incomparable beauty." However, the joy at having polished his work on the theory and submitting it was all the positivity there was in the letter.

He told Zangger was unhappy with David Hilbert the mathematician, the only person who seemed at the time to understand Einstein's theory, because it was apparent he had plagiarized his work. Just a week earlier, Hilbert had made a presentation in which he attempted to have a unified theory of gravity and electro-magnetism. In the paper he presented, he had incorporated Einstein's theory but did not seem to be giving credit where it was due.

Einstein was also upset about the situation with his family. He believed Mileva was trying to antagonism him and his children by maligning him. He explained to Zangger that his 11 year old son, Hans Albert, had not yet responded to confirm to Einstein if they were going to meet at a place in the Swiss Alps as Einstein had proposed. He spoke of the tender love that bound him and his kids, but told his friend that although the pain of separating from them initially pierced him like a dagger, he did not regret parting from their mother. In regards to being estranged from his children, he was extremely bitter. Zangger slightly outlived Einstein by two years, dying 1957.

Nicolai, Physiologist

George Friedlich Nicolai was a German physiologist who was born the same year as Einstein's other friend, Heinrich Zangger, 1874. He served as physiology professor at the University of Berlin from 1910, to 1915.

Like Albert Einstein, he was a pacifist, and the two of them even co-authored a manifesto that espoused pacifism entitled, Manifesto to Europeans.

That manifesto was meant to rebut another one, the Manifesto to the Civilized World, which had been signed by 93 German intellectuals. Among the eminent intellectuals of the period who had signed the latter were Wilhelm Rrntgen, Ernst Haeckel, Paul Ehrlich, and Max Planck.

The manifesto co-authored by Einstein and Nikolai was a plea to intellectuals to demand peace, and to proactively pursue the establishment of one united continent of Europe. The two friends took the manifesto that only two other colleagues, O. Bueck and W. J. Foerster, had signed, and they boldly circulated it amongst the professors at the University of Berlin. In their assessment, although most colleagues had not appended their signatures, many of them could relate to the document and had expressed their sympathy.

Pacifism was not something many people would have liked to associate with in the Germany of the day, considering how pro-war the country had been in that era. Thus, for the four colleagues to proactively promote it was a daring move. Because of his stance on the subject, Nikolai, who also worked as the family cardiologist for the royal family and as professor at the Berlin University, he lost both positions. He was also relieved of his position as Charite Hospital's Chief of Laboratory. In place of those prestigious positions, Nikolai was dispatched straight to Poland, which was known as Graundenz in those days, to become a garrison physician.

It was from that point of demotion that Nikolai managed to write The Biology of War. He managed to evade censorship of the book, and in 1916 it was published in Leipzig. Clearly, Einstein's radicalism was not without support. Nikolai faced a court martial in Danzig the same year, but he succeeded in making an escape for Denmark by plane towards the end of WWI. Luckily, too, when the Weimar Republic was established after WWI, Nikolai was reinstated back to his initial professional positions.

Unfortunately, there were strong right-wing sentiments within the university, particularly from a section of the students, and so the good physician decided to leave Germany for South America. For ten years, 1922–1932, he was a resident of Argentina, and from then on till his death in 1964, he lived in Chile. He had been doing well there as a member of faculty at the University of Chile, and he was even instrumental in establishing Chile's Phenomenological School of Psychiatry.

George Nikolai is one of the intellectuals who promoted the works of their friend, Albert Einstein. He is in a movie with the title, Der Einstein Film, which is on the relativity theory.

Mühsam, of the Jewish Hospital in Berlin

Albert Einstein and Hans Mühsam met in 1915 in Berlin. Mühsam was a medical doctor who had established a private practice after passing his medical examinations in 1900. At the same time, he became a member of staff at the city's Jewish Hospital. He was three years younger than Einstein, having been born in 1876. Like Einstein, he was born in Germany.

Einstein was little known among ordinary people in Berlin at the time he and Mühsam met. It happened that Elsa, Einstein's second wife, had a chance encounter with the family of Mühsam, during which time Mühsam remarked to Elsa that she bore a famous name. He even mentioned having heard of Albert Einstein.

When Elsa mentioned that encounter to Einstein, he became curious and he sought out the Mühsams. He got to meet them and almost instantly struck a friendship with Mühsam. They would go hiking together on Sundays, even as they discussed physics. They would also discuss issues of biological and medical nature. Their bond grew so strong that they even wrote a paper together on how to determine the permeability of filter papers. The close friendship that developed between Einstein and Mühsam was acknowledged and appreciated by both families. In fact that the paper Einstein wrote with Mühsam is his only one to grace a medical journal is in itself telling.

In a letter Mühsam's wife wrote to a person named, Seelig, after her husband's death, she recalls how during a certain period while in Berlin, Einstein would pay them a visit on a daily basis. She remembers a time when Einstein was trying to show her how close her husband was to him. To make it very clear that Einstein held Mühsam in high esteem, he had told his wife that her husband came first, then in a long space there was nothing, and only then did other people come to the picture.

There is ample evidence to indicate Mühsam was Einstein's confidante for the time they were both in Berlin. Einstein, who generally did not show any inclination to religion, is said to have confided in Mühsam that in his childhood, he would compose songs in praise of God, and then sing them on his way to school, even if nobody else was listening. Mühsam had then asked his friend how he thought things would have turned out for him if he had been born a Jew, but in a poor Russian family. Einstein's response was that he most probably would have become a Rabbi.

It was unfortunate that the two friends had to inevitably part ways, both bidding farewell to their homeland, Germany, and both for the same reason–the Nazi madness. While Einstein sought refuge in the U.S., Mühsam relocated to Israel where he lived a wizened man of eighty until 1957.

Chapter 25: Einstein's Scientific Achievements

Albert Einstein is indisputably famous. Arthur C. Clarke, a science writer, says Einstein's compact character that embodied humanism, pacifism, genius and even eccentricity made him the adored character that he was, and still is, today. And with the knowledge one now has of the man, these facets are in line with his general attitude towards life. Einstein did not wish to be boxed in anywhere, whether within a single religion, in an institution regimen, or in a marriage, too, unfortunately, or even in a country. He did not ask for freedom but demanded it and sought to acquire it the best way he knew how. In short, with Einstein, one can aptly say, had a self-emancipated mind.

Einstein's Year of Miracles

Einstein's prowess in science became concrete in 1905, the year of his famous, Annus Mirabilis, his four groundbreaking papers that were published in the Annalen der Physik, works that forthwith revolutionized the fundamentals of physics.

In one of those papers, Heuristic View of Light, which dealt with light emission and transformation, Einstein sought to explain the photoelectric effect by way of Planck's quantum hypothesis. Max Planck, the elder German physicist whom Einstein respected, described light as being a flow, comprising corpuscular objects that have definite energies. Planck had done an experiment with a magnet and conductor and come up with his theory, and it is that Electro-Dynamical theory that Einstein sought to modify.

Einstein's discovery was quite radical, as his explanation for the photoelectric effect deviated from what had been assumed in the 19th century regarding the light wave. Einstein explained that it was important to think of light as a stream made of particles or photons, and not as one whole single wave, which is what scientists assumed at the time. His discovery regarding light may have been radical, but it was a welcome relief for physicists who had observed unexplained results from prior experiments based on Planck's theory.

It was this wave theory of light that suggested that light could be considered a collection of particles, subsequently opening doors to the modern world of quantum physics. It was even the reason Einstein won the 1921 Nobel Prize in Physics.

In another of those papers, Einstein sought to explain the random movement of small particles in otherwise stationary liquids. In the Wave Theory, electrons are expected to be ejected with extra energy whenever there is increased incident light. However, experiments tended to show energies as being entirely independent of the intensity of radiation. Einstein brought a better understanding of the photoelectric effect, showing precisely how electrons get ejected from a metal surface as a result of incident light. As would be expected, many scientists found it difficult to accept that the theory they had relied upon for so long could have had deficiencies, but considering how factual science is, they soon accepted Einstein's theory and found it helpful.

Einstein's Theory of Special Relativity

When it comes to the Special Relativity Theory, Albert Einstein demonstrated that all observers find physical laws identical, the only condition being that none of them is under acceleration at the time. What stands out, according to Einstein's discovery, is the speed of light through a vacuum because whether an observer is moving slowly or fast, it remains the same.

Einstein's Special Relativity With Regards To Space and Time

Einstein importantly found the link between space and time, now generally referred to as space-time. Einstein showed that it was important to replace absolute time with an entirely new absolute, which was the speed of light. He ignored the physics that was viewed as being conventional in his day, and visualized a universe where the two elements, space and time, were relative. He also visualized a universe where light speed was absolute. In the days before Einstein's discovery, scientists held the belief that space and time were the absolute factors, while light was the relative one. From the space-time link, there came a unique realization that an observer could witness an event at a particular time, and the same event could be witnessed by another observer at an entirely different time.

In order to easily comprehend Einstein's unification of space and time, one needs to view the universe as possessing three space dimensions–the up and down dimension, the left and right dimension, and the forward and backward dimension. Then there is the one time dimension that makes the fourth. When these dimensions are considered together as a 4-dimensional space, it is termed the space-time continuum.

Another way of looking at the application of this theory Einstein came up with is by way of checking out two points, which happen to be moving at speeds that are constant relative to one another; what Einstein refers to as varying inertia frames of reference. This theory enables the observer to interpret that motion in between those points. Einstein explains the state of those moving objects as relative motion as opposed to it appealing to the atmosphere the way an absolute frame of reference would to define whatever is happening.

As far as Einstein's theory goes, when two people are moving through space, one at a high speed, and the other one at a much slower speed, each of them makes different observations regarding space and time.

In expounding the theory, Einstein said that if two astronauts were trying to compare their observations, yet each of them was in a different spaceship, the only thing that would be of consequence would be how fast they were moving relative to each other. It is important to note that special relatively only applies in cases where the motion being considered is uniform, which is the reason the term, special, is used. The other assumption is that the person making the observation is not traveling zigzag, but in a straight line, and also at a speed that is constant.

In short, if the observer reaches a point and alters the nature of the motion, for example, moves in a curve or accelerates, special relativity is no longer applicable. However, Einstein the brilliant scientist, did not leave the problem he observed pending. This scenario where the motion has been varied in speed and direction can be explained by his General Theory of Relativity, which actually has the capacity to explain motion of any sort.

Einstein's Basic Relativity Principles

Einstein's Special Relativity Theory is based primarily on two principles:

(i)   The relativity principle

Under this principle, physics laws remain unchanged, and that includes laws related to objects moving at constant speed from the frame of reference, what can also be referred to as objects moving in frames of reference that are inertial.

(ii)   The speed of light principle

For every observer, the speed of light happens to be the same under this principle, and that is irrespective of their motion in relation to the source of light. When physicists are writing down this speed, they use the symbol c.

Einstein's Genius

What ended up distinguishing Einstein from other physicists was that he conducted his experiments with an open mind. Unlike other scientists, who, having knowledge of other theories, did experiments expecting to satisfy such theories, and when they failed they took their experiments to have been wrongly done, Einstein did the reverse. He conducted his experiments and trusted their results. Then he sought to establish on what counts those results varied from those stipulated by the existing theory or theories.

As such, he had no qualms terming a theory wrong if by his experiment it did not work as presupposed. It was just the same way he seemed to relate liberally in other spheres of life. He was never one to like rules that inhibited his exploration.

Towards the end of the 19th century, the item that inhibited scientists, and which Einstein decided to ignore in order to make free observations, and deductions of his own, was something called ether–a medium of sorts. Scientists believed that ether existed, and it was through it that light waves traveled. According to Einstein, the presumption of the existence of ether and its role in light travel was an unnecessary inhibition and simply a mess. He did not see why the medium, ether, should be introduced into the equation, so that some physics laws worked differently according to the movement of the observer relative to the medium.

What Einstein did was to discard the idea of ether, and then conducted his experiments on the assumption that all the laws of physics, inclusive of the one of speed of light, worked always the same way, irrespective of how the observer was moving. After all, Einstein observed, it was the same for the laws in mathematics; his experiments supported that premise.

Einstein's Theory of General Relativity

As for the General Relativity Theory, it was simply the earlier law of gravity reformulated, but in a significantly radical way. The law of gravity was originally formulated by Isaac Newton in the 1600s, and in it he explained how the force of gravity affected two bodies. According to Newton, the force affecting the two bodies depended on the mass of each of those two bodies, and the distance between them. However, to Einstein, one needed to take space-time into account, hence to appreciate how relative the force is.

Einstein demonstrated that gravity is manifested when an object drops into a kind of well that is created by some space-time distortion. In explaining the space-time distortion that gives the impression of a massive object, Einstein used the analogy of a heavy ball being placed on some trampoline.

Einstein's Unified Field Theory

Another of Einstein's great theories was Unified Field Theory. In this theory, he tried to link the fields of electromagnetism and gravity, however, without real success. Nevertheless, considering scientists only came to understand better the concept of quantum mechanics in the 1970s and 1980s, the Encyclopedia Britannica reckons Einstein was actually ahead of his time. In fact, physicists after him have taken up his unsuccessful endeavor in earnest, with the hope they will be able to explain what the great physicist tried to for many years.

How Einstein's Work Has Been Applied

Einstein's work, though highly scientific, was based on daily occurrences. When it comes to light or gravity, for example, these are factors that affect daily lives; however, one does not consciously think about them. Still, there are some instances where Einstein's theories have been applied or proven over again, and they have either made major impact on other aspects of science or made it easier to understand and explain other facets of science.

Gravitational Waves

One hundred years after Albert Einstein forecast the existence of space-time ripples as an aspect of his General Relativity Theory, in 2015, the Laser Interferometer Gravitational-wave Observatory (LIGO) detected gravitational waves. A year later, the same body detected the space-time ripples Einstein had predicted, also referred to as gravitational waves. LIGO established the waves had occurred after a collision of black holes, a distance of around 1.4 billion light years from earth. A light year is the distance that light travels within a period of a year, at that same constant speed. A single light year is essentially 5,878 billion miles or 9.46 x 1015 meters.

Mercury's Orbit

The issue of mercury's orbit is another area that physicists could not comprehend properly, especially because it is a relatively small planet, and it orbits in very close proximity to a relatively massive object, the sun. The Theory of General Relativity enabled scientists to understand the scenario, showing how the space-time curvature affects the motions of Mercury and alters its orbit.

Scientists have also being able to deduce, based on the same theory, that there is a slim chance that one day, over billions of years, the small planet could be ejected out of the solar system due to orbital changes. They have also been able to deduce, similarly by virtue of this theory by Einstein, that there is an even smaller chance that this small planet could one day collide with planet earth.

Gravitational Lensing

Scientists have now been able to observe objects they would not have understood were it not for Einstein's theory on light travel. Gravitational lensing is the phenomenon by which a huge object bends light around it, thus enabling the observer to see an object behind it. Examples of such massive objects include a galaxy, a black hole, or even a cluster. Once astrologers look at such an object using a telescope, they are able to see objects that are right behind the huge object, courtesy of the bent light.

Einstein exemplified this phenomenon with a gravitationally lensed quasar within the Pegasus constellation, commonly referred to as the Einstein Cross. In this case, a galaxy that is around 400 million light years far off bends light emanating from quasar, and as a result the quasar is seen to be present at four different locations around the galaxy.

Chapter 26: Other Major Achievements

There are so many exemplary things that Albert Einstein did in his life that impacted the way physics is tackled today, but because he did others that were revolutionary in a monumental way, others are often ignored.

1. Einstein substantiated the atomic theory with empirical evidence

In science, nothing is credible until it can be demonstrated empirically, thus the fact that Einstein was able to prove the atomic theory in this manner gives him a place in science aside from other achievements. As usual, he was observant even in ordinary situations, and he let his mind think liberally, not afraid to accept results that tended to dismantle the status quo. He was also persistent in his pursuits.

In this instance, he picked up an observation that a fellow scientist before him, Robert Brown had, and worked on it to its logical conclusion. Brown had watched water that had pollen grains in it using a microscope, and he made the observation that the pollen grains were moving through the water. That was in 1827. What he did not establish was the mechanism by which the pollen grains were moving around in the water, or the reason for the motion. Einstein did.

In a 1905 paper, Einstein wrote what he termed Brownian motion. From his own observation he could see that the movement of the tiny grains in the liquid was random, and he also knew of the possible existence of atoms and molecules. His explanation in the published paper was that the individual pollen grains were being set in motion by various water molecules. Einstein's explanation not only gave a credible explanation to the random movement of particles in a liquid, but it also gave confirmation to the existence of atoms and molecules.

Essentially, Einstein's work culminating in the Brownian motion of particles reflected great insight. He took kinetic theory ideas and classical hydrodynamics and blended them, and hence he was able to derive the mean free path equation of such particles being a function of time.

2. He facilitated determination of the Avogadro's number

Einstein put a lot of work into the paper on Brownian motion, just as he did for his other papers. This led to the determination of how big molecules are, by establishing how big atoms are. And since a mole is made up of atoms, he is credited with facilitating the experiment that determined the Avogadro's number, and subsequently the exact number of atoms in a single molecule. It is his statistical analysis of the behavior of atoms that provided other scientists a lead as to the best way to count atoms by simply observing them through a microscope.

3. Einstein solved the photoelectric riddle

Photoelectric effect means electron emissions from metallic material that result once light has been shone on it. The closest theory scientists could have tried to use was Maxwell's Light Wave Theory, but it did not help. However, in Einstein's paper of June 9, 1905, which is deemed revolutionary, he challenged Light Wave Theory, suggesting that light be taken to be an assembly of discrete energy packets, otherwise called photons.

This particle theory of light by Einstein was at first rejected by fellow physicists, but it was verified ten years later through experiments by Robert Andrew Millikan, the 1923 Nobel Prize winner for physics. Einstein's scientific discovery was instrumental in establishing the quantum mechanics field, and quantum mechanics was subsequently responsible for explaining numerous features of the universe. In fact, quantum mechanics is widely used in inventions of modern technology.

4. Inconsistencies in the Newtonian mechanics

Not only did Einstein identify inconsistencies in the mechanics of Isaac Newton, he found a way to rectify them. It was the mechanics of Isaac Newton and the electromagnetism equations of Maxwell Planck that prompted Einstein to work on his renowned paper, On the Electrodynamics of Moving Bodies, published in September 1905. According to Einstein, whenever the situation being handled is near the speed of light, it is important to make big changes in the mechanics. This was the argument that was gradually developed to become Special Relativity Theory, and which was well supported and confirmed using experimental evidence. Soon, the theory gained general acceptance, and in today's world it is deemed the most accurate motion model whenever speed is involved.

5. The rest energy concept

There is an equation famously linked to Einstein, and that is E=mc2. E in the equation stands for energy, while m represents mass. C is representative of the speed of light within a vacuum. Einstein created this equation to affirm the mass-energy equivalence.

What has not been mentioned in earlier chapters is that it is in formulating this equation that Einstein demonstrated that a particle has some form of energy, quite separate from the already known kinetic and potential energies, what he termed rest energy. By implication, therefore, gravity has the capacity to bend light in a way that can be used to determine the amount of energy that has been released, or even consumed, in instances of nuclear reactions.

6. General Relativity Theory

While it is not news that Einstein formulated the General Theory of Relativity, it is important to mention the impact of the theory that sought to generalize Newton's universal gravitational law, even as it generalized special relativity. It provided a description of gravity in a unified way, representing it as a space and time geometric property, or simply space-time.

The general relativity concept helped model the universe' massive structure, and whatever predictions it produced have been confirmed by actual observations and experiments over time. Today, the theory is applied in modern astrophysics as a major tool to enable understanding of various phenomena, such as black holes, and even gravitational lensing.

Einstein's mind was constantly at work. When he noticed areas where his special relativity theory had limitations, he did more work that led to the publication of his 1915 paper on general relativity. The concepts he came up with were greatly thought out, yet this second paper at first attracted a lot of controversy.

One of the admirable characteristics of Einstein was his tenacity and self-belief. He was not one to be disillusioned just because other people were skeptical of his findings. As long as he knew his experiments were accurate and his reasoning logical, he stuck to his guns.

The paper he later published in 1917 is testament to this trait. In that work, Einstein utilized the concept of general relativity in modeling the behavior of the universe as a whole. General relativity has ended up spreading across all spheres of life, and even more prominently in the area of modern astronomy.

7. Bose-Einstein condensate

Einstein was a good team player whenever an opportunity availed itself, as has been seen in his earlier collaboration in papers with his friend, Grossman. In this instance, Einstein collaborated with Satyendra Nath Bose, who was an Indian physicist, to predict the existence of a condensate that was to later gain popularity as the Bose-Einstein condensate. Bose had originated a paper in 1924, which bore a counting method, with an assumption that one could take light to be some form of gas with indistinguishable particles.

Bose had actually approached Einstein with his short paper that described light as comprising a gas of photons, and all he wanted at the time was help in getting the paper published. As Einstein went through the paper, it dawned on him that it was possible to apply the very same statistics to atoms.

Einstein got the paper published in a journal after it had been translated to German. He also prepared an article that he also got published in German, in which he described Bose's model and included explanations about the implications it had. Later the two physicists worked on the concept further and expanded it to incorporate the atom aspect. Following the Bose-Einstein statistics, any assembly of the indistinguishable particles is referred to as bosons.

It was this extended work that led to the prediction that a condensate phenomena existed. Many decades passed by, and it was only in 1995 that the said condensate was experimentally produced. One thing to note is that in the days of Einstein, German was the lingua franca in the field of physics.

8. Quantum Mechanics

Einstein engaged in scientific debates with his fellow physicist, Niels Bohr, and they ended up with the quantum mechanics used today. The sequence of public debates the two scientists were involved in had a great impact on the general philosophy of science, and they marked the highest level of scientific research early 20th century had seen. Most importantly, they brought to the fore the idea of quantum non-locality, which is essentially part of the quantum theory. That particular quantum theory aspect is fundamental to today's comprehension of the physical universe.

9. Photoelectric Effect Law

Even for someone who has no idea what Albert Einstein did to warrant fame, there is still the Nobel Prize to elevate him to the platform of who's who. He was nominated for the prize in the physics category in 1920, but due to some pressure on the committee concerned, which was going on behind the scenes, courtesy of Einstein's political stance, he was not announced the winner then. However, the integrity of the committee stood the test, and in 1921, Einstein was awarded the prize together with the year's winner; thus two Nobel Prizes for physics were presented in the same year.

The outstanding scientific work that led to this global recognition of Einstein was generally in theoretical physics, and specifically the part that resulted in his discovery of Photoelectric Effect Law. Even the Royal Society honored him with the Copley Medal, one of the most ancient scientific awards that were still being offered.

Einstein also ended up receiving many more awards for that groundbreaking scientific work, including the Franklin Medal, which he was awarded in 1935. Earlier on in 1921, he had received the Matteucci Medal; Gold Medal of the Royal Astronomical Society, which he was awarded in 1926; the Max Planck Medal that came in 1929; and thereafter, in 1935, the Franklin Medal. Decades later, in 1999, Albert Einstein was named the Person of the Century by the respected Time Magazine.

10. His mark on everyday life

People may not have recognized the full implication of Einstein's discoveries and analysis, but they certainly have had tremendous impact on modern daily life. Many of the successes in modern technology and scientific innovation have been possible because Einstein observed and discovered very fundamental aspects of science. Some good examples of technical areas that have benefitted from Einstein's work include the production of nuclear energy and GPS satellite synchronization.

11. Why the sky is blue

Einstein's work culminating in the Brownian motion of particles reflected great insight. He took kinetic theory ideas and classical hydrodynamics and blended them, and hence he was able to derive the mean free path equation of such particles being a function of time.

12. Dark Matter

Einstein and a Dutch physicist, De Sitter, who was also a mathematician and astronomer, came up with propositions on how to solve the general relativity field equations. De Sitter was seven years older than Einstein. The two also suggested the existence of massive amounts of matter without the capacity to emit light, and which are yet to be detected. True to their suggestion, just by monitoring gravitational effects, such matter has been seen to exist. Scientists have given it the term dark matter.

13. Einstein-de Sitter Model

Albert Einstein and de Sitter also worked together in 1932, and the two came up with a unique model today referred to as the Einstein-de Sitter Model. This model is dominated by the Friedmann Model that has zero curvature, meaning k = 0. It also corresponds to the Minkowski Universe, also with zero curvature. In the Einstein-de Sitter model, the universe is bound to continue expanding infinitely, and with the right energy amount, it could escape to infinity. Their prediction is analogous with the situation of launching a rocket.

In the latter situation, all a rocket requires is for its energy to exceed a given critical velocity, which can be termed escape velocity, and it will find itself continuing in space with its speed ever-increasing. Of course, in a situation where the rocket is provided with insufficient energy, it would find itself being pulled back towards the earth. However, in a situation where the rocket is at the exact escape velocity, it is bound to continue escaping the earth, but its velocity will be rescinding to zero as the rocket nears spatial infinity.

This Einstein-de Sitter Model matches the one of the universe, where the universe would have the right escape velocity as the one provided by the Big Bang, enabling it escape the gravity pull, and that owing to the matter within the universe.

Chapter 27: Various Proofs of the Validity of Einstein's Laws

One person can observe, analyze and understand a phenomenon, but until an independent mind follows the person's logic and confirms it to be true, it cannot pass as a law. It more or less remains the original person's hypothesis, and other people can work with it on that basis. For Einstein, it means there is a lot he observed, analyzed and understood that fellow scientists confirmed to be valid. Establishing how natural phenomena operates is no mean task, and it is no wonder not many experts come up with more than a single law in their lifetime.

It is, therefore, natural that people should marvel at the brilliance of Einstein to the level of terming him a genius. It may not have been easy for fellow scientists to get into his mindset and succeed in viewing, for instance, the aspect of space-time, a factor that is not measurable in conventional ways, such as by use of scientific instruments, but they did ultimately appreciate it. Better still, by warping space-time, scientists have been able to make predictions, with the predicted phenomena materializing and turning out to be correct.

How Gravitational Lensing Works

In gravitational lensing, light surrounding a huge object is bent, and that makes it function as a lens. In that capacity, the bent light enables visibility of the items lying behind the huge object. The discovery that Einstein made years ago has had a positive impact in air explorations and other spheres of science in a monumental way. It is on its basis, for example, that astronomers are able to study stars in a way that has today become routine. They are also able to observe and study galaxies that lie behind enormous objects, courtesy of Einstein's gravitational lensing.

There are instances where astronomers have observed a massive black hole ejecting energy from right inside a galaxy, and owing to Einstein's discovery, the astronomers are able to appreciate the scenario when the black hole plays the role of a cosmic lens or magnifying glass. It then allows them to have a vivid picture of far off objects, including galaxies much more far off. In fact, because of this scientific discovery of bending light and how it impacts visualization, astronomers are able to observe more than one galaxy at a time.

Another good example of gravitational lensing is the quasar that is often referred to as Einstein's Cross. This quasar is located around 8 billion light years away from the earth, right behind a galaxy that happens to be 400 million light years further. When observed, one sees four images of the quasar, all appearing around the far off galaxy. The reason for this image is that the light from the quasar is being bent by the gravity intensity of the galaxy.

Einstein's was a groundbreaking discovery as far as the impact of light being bent is concerned, and scientists have over the years used the discovery to further their scientific explorations. Their work has impacted the way the world works, including the world of travel and space explorations, but, in most cases, what has been observed are objects that are, for most part, static. However, this trend appears set to change, as scientists have begun to observe objects that are in motion.

Such observations are bound to have implications on the way scientific principles have been applied in understanding other phenomena. In short, the world of science is going to continue changing as more phenomena are understood, courtesy of gravitational lensing. Consequently, people are bound to continue experiencing more modernization changes as scientists increase their knowledge and understanding.

Back to the lens, considering that light traveling around that lens moves along a different path, and all the rays travel over varying amounts of time, scientists have been able to acknowledge a supernova that happened to appear four different times. These appearances were a result of the magnification of the supernova by an enormous galaxy.

In March 2015, scientists reported having observed for the first time a celestial magnifying glass that allowed them to observe an explosion of a single star four times. It was thought this would provide a better understanding of the explosive astral deaths, as well as the nature of earth's acceleration.

Astronomers used the Hubble Space Telescope to capture the supernova's four images, following its explosion within deep space. This successful observation was attributed to the galaxy that lay between the earth and that particular star that exploded. The image displayed through the telescope was a result of the galaxy cluster warping the space fabric and time all around it, and as explained by experts, it was just like a bowling ball being placed on some bed sheet, thus enabling the watching scientists to observe the four images of the supernova.

An astronomer based at the University of California, Patrick Kelly, said at the time that the possibility of a supernova being gravitationally lensed the way it happened had been predicted half a century before, but for so long no one had been able to identify such an incident. He expressed excitement that they were able to find the very first example of gravitational lensing happening. Such joy is understandable, considering the reason a theory or law is held in such high regard is that other scholars can use it with full confidence that results it is based on will be valid.

Such an example goes to confirm that Einstein's work did not comprise empty scholarly pieces of work, but credible work that became the basis of quality work that is meant to advance the quality of life of humankind. In this first sighting of the four images of a single supernova, for example, reputable bodies interested in scientific research and advancement was piqued. Such bodies included the European Space Agency (ESA), National Aeronautics and Space Administration

(NASA), Space Telescope Science Institute and universities, such as Johns Hopkins and University of California, Berkeley.

Supernova Sighted in Gravitational Lensing

The supernova that provided the historic observation and further validation of Einstein's work was first seen in November 2014, and its distance was estimated to be 9.3 billion light years from the earth. It was also observed that its location was close to the edge of the space of the universe within sight.

The name researchers gave to the supernova was SN Refsdal, and it was in honor of a Norwegian astrophysicist called Sjur Refsdal, who, before his death, was in the pioneer group of scientists whp were heavily involved in the studies involving gravitational lensing. Jens Hjorth, who is head of Dark Cosmology Centre that is part of University of Copenhagen's Niels Bohr Institute, explained that the brightness of the supernova seems to be 20 times greater than normal because of gravitational lensing.

In this particular instance, the lensing galaxy involved is around 5 billion light years away from the earth, and it is not in isolation. Rather, it is part of a massive galaxy cluster, referred to as MACS J1149.6+2223. Back in 2009, astronomers had found out that the cluster originated the largest spiral galaxy image ever observed by way of a gravitational lens.

One aspect that amazed the scientists was that the four supernova images emerged at varying times and not concurrently. Their sighting was actually over a period of weeks. The reason for the varying times of sighting, according to experts, is that light has the capacity to travel through different paths, moving around and ultimately through the gravitational lens to reach the earth at varying times.

How to Use Gravity as a Lens

In any instance where the fabric of reality is warped by matter, gravity is made, and the bigger the object mass, the higher the incident of space-time curving around that particular object. Along the same lines, the stronger the gravitational pull of the object is based on the discovery Einstein made in the Theory of General Relativity.

Consequently, gravity has the capacity to bend light the same way a lens does. This essentially means it is possible to view objects that lie behind strong gravitational fields in large sizes, as exemplified by those of massive galaxies. The very first time gravitational lensing was discovered was 1979, and in the modern day, it is normal for astronomers to use it in observing features that would normally prove too distant to detect, or to see clearly. In the absence of gravitational lensing, even very large telescopes would not be helpful in viewing such objects.

In Kelly's explanation, gravitational lenses operate just like any magnifying glass; only this one is natural. He notes that the magnifications of the gravitational lenses as one looks through galaxy clusters can be up to a hundred times. He further explains that there is weak lensing whenever the relevant gravitational lensing mass is not particularly large, or when the light being bent is too far away from the mass. This is because the light is barely distorted.

On the contrary, there is strong lensing whenever light emerges from right behind the relevant gravitational lensing mass, or at least, close by. Scientists have noted that whenever there is a strong lensed object occupying a massive patch of space like a galaxy, it is possible for it to be smeared into what is known as Einstein's Ring, which surrounds a particular gravitationally lensing mass. This is different when it comes to small items that are point-like, such as quasars that are known to be super bright. Their strong lensing is generally known to produce several images, and they all surround the gravitational lensing mass with the resultant Einstein Cross.

SN Refsdal's observations have been marked as the very first time astronomers have witnessed a significantly strong supernova lensing from their position on earth, with four clear images of a star in an explosion spread in an array to form an Einstein's cross.

Einstein's Cross

Einstein's Cross, which in scientific lingo is represented by Q2237+030 or QSO 2237+0305, means the gravitationally lensed quasar that is seated right behind galaxy ZW 2237+030, otherwise referred to as Huchra's Lens. It is formed by four images of the quasar, with an additional similar image positioned right in the middle of the shape formed by the other four. Of course, Einstein's Cross, being so far away cannot be seen by the naked eye, and even astronomers use modern telescopes for that.

Chapter 28: Einstein's Life Away from Physics

Albert Einstein's birth is recorded as Mar 14, 1879 at 11.30 AM in Ulm, Germany. He was the son of Pauline and Hermann Einstein. His family relocated to Munich in June of the following year. While in Munich, Albert welcomed a sister, Maria, who was born on November 18, 1881. She was popularly referred to as Maja.

Einstein began receiving private lessons in 1884 to prepare him for school, and it was during that time that his father showed him the much talked about compass that piqued his curiosity in physics. This compass is often referred to as Einstein's first wonder. From October 1885, Einstein began attending Petersschule, a Catholic based elementary school within Munich, and he was seen to be generally a good pupil. His parents had him receive Jewish religious lessons at home. During this time, young Einstein developed interest in the violin, and he began to learn how to play it.

From October 1, 1888, Einstein no longer attended Petersshule, but instead began learning at Luitpold-Gymnasium, the equivalent of a grammar school. His curiosity in different phenomena was gradually rising, and the following year he was glad to meet Max Talmund, whose name later changed to Talmey. Talmund, like Einstein, was Jewish, and he had come to study medicine in Germany. Talmud and young Einstein read books together and discussed a wide range of topics, most of them relating to science and philosophy. Talmud actually served as Einstein's tutor during that time. He even introduced him to a book that interested him a lot, and which Einstein preferred to call the holy geometry book. That was young Einstein's second wonder after the compass.

As Einstein reveled at the content of the geometry book, he was also engrossed in religious learning. He had a teacher, as well as a rabbi, preparing him for Bar Mitzvah, the rite of passage conducted for Jewish boys at the age of 13. By the time he was of age, he had begun to become weary of the confinement of religion, and not wishing to be limited in his thinking and his beliefs, he skipped the Bar Mitzvah ceremony. He was now a fully - fledged free thinker.

While Einstein was still a student at Luitpold-Gymnasium, his parents decided to relocate to Milan in Italy because his father wanted to try business elsewhere. In Munich, the business he was operating with his brother was not doing well. Hence, the family left Einstein behind in 1894 to continue his learning, instead of interrupting his secondary school education. Soon, Hermann, Einstein's father, was to relocate with his immediate family to Pavia, still in Italy, where he decided to go it alone in business, although still he later returned to Milan.

When Einstein was left to pursue the last part of his secondary school course, he was uncomfortable and only stayed for some months. In December the same year his family left, he conned his way out of school and joined them to Pavia.

In October 1895, Einstein tried to join the Swiss Technical College, or ETH, also referred to sometimes as the Swiss Polytechnic. However, he did not pass the entrance examination. Since he had performed exemplarily in some subjects, such as math and physics, the principal advised him to stick around, instead of returning to Italy, and prepare to try again.

Einstein stayed with a large family in Aarau, where he was doing his preparations by attending secondary school to catch up with what he had lost in Munich. The family that hosted Einstein from late October when he began school was headed by Professor Jost Winteler. It was during this period that Einstein's closed personality seemed to change. He soon became social and even entered into his first romantic relationship with one of Professor Winteler's daughters.

In 1896, when Einstein was 17yrs old, he gave up German citizenship and declared he no longer belonged to Württemberg, the kingdom that ended in 1918. He had his father's blessings as he did so, and for five years Einstein did not belong to any state.

When in October of 1896, the results of the Matura were released in Aarau, he had passed. The Matura was the basic qualification for university entry. He joined Zurich Polytechnic that same October, and he was very eager to pursue mathematics and physics. They were actually the subjects he specialized in as he trained to be a teacher. It is at the Polytechnic that he met his future wife, Mileva Maric, and one of his lifetime friends, Marcel Grossman.

In 1897, Einstein met another lifetime friend, Michele Besso, in Zurich, and in 1899, while in Zurich, he applied to become a Swiss citizen. Einstein's courses led to his qualification as a teacher, with a diploma in Mathematics and Physics. He applied to join the same polytechnic as an assistant but was unsuccessful. His failure had little, if anything, to do with his competence, but rather his poor relationship with some influential lecturers at the college.

In February 1900, Einstein's application for Swiss citizenship was approved. With his persistent application for an assistant's job at the Polytechnic and various universities consistently failing, he took up a temporary job as a teacher in Winterthur, Switzerland, where he taught from May up to July. From September the same year, he taught in Schaffhausen, still in Switzerland, at a private school. In December, he applied to work in Bern at the Swiss Patent Office, and Marcel Grossmann, his college friend, helped him to secure it.

In January 1902, Einstein's daughter with his college girlfriend, Mileva Maric, was born. Although the two were not married at the time, Einstein decided on the responsibility of taking care of mother and daughter, and he began advertising to offer private classes. Finally, in June 23, 1902, he was employed at the Patent Office as a 3rd class technical expert. His work station was in Bern. Unfortunately, in October of the same year, Einstein lost his father, Hermann, to illness. In fact, he dashed to see him at his bedside when he learned he was very ill. In January 1903, Einstein married his girlfriend, Maric, although parents from both sides did not favor the marriage. Maric did not even bring her daughter with her when she joined Einstein in Bern, but instead left her with her parents in Hungary. It is believed that the daughter was given up for adoption there in Hungary in the autumn of 1903. The couple had their first son while in Bern on May 14, 1904, and they named him Hans Albert. In the meantime, Einstein was offered a permanent job at the Patent Office. Now that he was well settled as a family man and had a stable job, he began his academic and scientific pursuit. Once he began getting serious papers published in 1905, it was science work non-stop until his death in 1955.

Along the way, on July 28, 1910, he and Maric had their second son whom they named Eduard. In 1912, Einstein began an extramarital affair with his cousin, Elsa Löwenthal, who still lived in Berlin, Germany. By 1914, Einstein had become highly sought after, and in April he relocated to Berlin. His wife and children followed him in May the same year. His marriage had now become strained, and he and Maric decided to part ways. In July, Maric took the children with her to Zurich where she continued to take care of them until they were grown up.

Unfortunately, WWI had been looming, and it broke out on August 1, 1914. Einstein took a few months' break from his scientific work to participate in politics in his own way. He joined Bund Neues Vaterland as a pacifist, even signing the manifesto addressed to the Europeans, Manifest an die Europäer. He had partnered in designing the manifesto with Georg Nikolai and Fritz Haber.

1917 was not a good year for Einstein health-wise. He suffered various ailments, including one that affected his liver, as well as a stomach ulcer. It took him a long time to heal properly, although his cousin and lover took care of him. The following year, Einstein was happy when, in November, the German Reich surrendered and the Weimar Republic was declared.

Einstein and Maric's divorce came through on Feb 14, 1919, and on June 2 the same year, Einstein married Elsa Löwenthal. She immediately moved in with Einstein and brought her daughters, Ilse and Margot, from her previous marriage to live with them. In the meantime, Einstein was having discussions on Zionism with Kurt Blumenfeld. In addition, Einstein lost his mother, Pauline, in February 1920 to illness. She lived in Berlin at the time.

Chaim Weizmann got Einstein to accompany him to the U.S., a trip that began on April 2, 1921 and that ended on May 30 the same year. It was the first time Einstein had set foot in the U.S., and the purpose was raise to funds for establishing a university in Jerusalem–the Hebrew University. The following year in January, Einstein visited Prague and Vienna, and in April he visited France. He gave speeches during those visits, and they served to normalize the relationship between Germany and France that had become very strained after WWI.

On June 24, 1922, Walther Rathenau, who served as Germany's Foreign Secretary, was assassinated, and Einstein canceled his scheduled public appearances in his honor. He even wrote a great piece for his obituary. On October 8 the same year, he and his wife set out for a long journey that would take them to Japan, Colombo, and even Singapore, Hong Kong, and Shanghai.

In February 1923, Einstein and his wife traveled to Palestine as they made their way back from the Japan trip, and there he became the first person to be made Tel Aviv's honorary citizen. They also stopped to visit Spain.

Beginning April 1925 all through to June, Einstein undertook a journey that saw him visit the South American countries of Argentina, Uruguay, and Brazil. In the same year, he, Mahatma Gandhi, and other eminent persons signed a manifesto denouncing compulsory military service. During the same year, he joined the Hebrew University's administrative council.

In 1928, Einstein was again down with ill health, this time very likely due to over-exertion. He had a heart ailment that kept him bedridden for months, and which took almost a year to heal. On April 13 the same year, Helen Dukas began to work for him as a secretary. She was later to become his housekeeper as well when his second wife died.

In March 1929, Einstein celebrated his 50th birthday, and in the same year he built a family house in Caputh, Germany.

In 1930, Einstein's son, Hans Albert, along with his wife, Frieda, had their firstborn, thus Einstein had his first grandson. They named him Bernhard Caesar. In May of the same year, Einstein took part in signing a manifesto that demanded that countries get rid of heavy armament, even as he got deeper into pacifism.

In March 1932, Einstein returned to Germany from the U.S., but he decides to pursue the invitation he had received earlier to join the anticipated institute at Princeton. During the same year, he began to write as a co-author with Sigmund Freud, an Austrian psychologist, and their topic was why countries went to war. Their work was published in 1933.

In December 1932, Einstein traveled to Pasadena, California, from Berlin, to lecture at CalTech in the U.S., and although his return journey was planned for March 1933, the Nazis rose to power in January 1933, and the political climate became bad for him. In March 1933, Einstein cuts ties with all the German institutes with whom he was associated, including the Prussian Academy.

In 1934, Einstein lost his stepdaughter, Ilse, who died in Paris, and in the same year his other stepdaughter, Margot came to Princeton to live with him. To bring some sunshine to his year, his collection of non-scientific work, titled Mein Weltbild, or The World as I See It was published.

In September 1935, Einstein, Elsa, Margot and his secretary, Helen Dukas, moved in together to occupy

Einstein's new house at Mercer Street 112, Princeton. In 1936, Einstein lost his great friend, Marcel Grossman, who died on September 7, and in the same year he lost his wife, Elsa, who passed away on December 20.

In 1943, Einstein was sought by the U.S. Navy to serve as advisor in relation to highly explosive materials. However, in 1945, when the US bombed Hiroshima and Nagasaki, Einstein was devastated. Those two bombings marked the end of WWII, but according to Einstein, although the war had been won, peace had not been attained, and he said so during a dinner to commemorate his Nobel Prize that December in New York.

In 1946, Einstein wrote an open letter to the UN, mainly promoting the idea of a unified world government. He was also chosen to head a committee of atomic scientists mandated to control armament and provide guidance on safe use of nuclear energy. The following year, he persisted to promote pacifism and the idea of a single world government.

1948 was not good for him, as it was the year Mileva Maric died in August, and he was diagnosed with a massive aorta aneurysm, for which he received immediate surgery. He was discharged from hospital in January the following year. In March 1950, Einstein finalized his will and nominated Dr. Otto Nathan as well as Helen Dukas his administrators. In 1951, Einstein lost his only sister, Maja, who died on June 25.

In 1952, Einstein was honored by being offered he Israel presidency, after the demise of his friend, Chaim Weizmann, but he politely declined, declaring he did not deem himself fit for the position. In 1954 he showed open support for his fellow Jew physicist, J.R. Oppenheimer, whom the US government had accused of being a security risk.

In the same year, Einstein suffered hemolytic anemia. In April 1955, Einstein fell ill after his aneurysm burst, and he was admitted at a Princeton hospital on April 15. However, despite treatment, he died at around 1:15am on April 18 at the age of 76.

Chapter 29: Einstein's Prolific Scientific Journey

In 1889, Einstein was introduced to Critique of Pure Reason, the so-called Einstein's holy geometry, and Euclid's elements by Kant. It was from Euclid that he began to appreciate deductive reasoning, which is very crucial in theoretical physics. When at the age of 12 he came across a booklet in school that contained Euclidean geometry, he was much interested in reading it and began to find out more about calculus.

Euclid is the name of a Greek mathematician who lived in 300 BC, and who wrote 13 books covering topics on various elements, later termed Euclid's elements. Those elements include definitions, theorems relating to geometry, and others.

Einstein is said to have written his first work of a scientific nature before he was 17, specifically during his stay in Aarau. However, he did not have any work published until March 1901, when the scientific work he had submitted in December 1900 to the Annalen der Physik, or Annals of Physics, was published.

Since he was very interested in brainstorming about science, he formed the Akademie Olympia, or Olympics Academy in 1903, which was comprised of him and some Bern friends, Maurice Solovine and Gesellschaft. In May the same year, he acquired membership into Bern's Naturforschende Gesellschaft, or Naturalist Society.

1905 was Einstein's most prolific year, the annus mirabilis, what people generally termed his year of miracles. He published his four major papers in close sequence in the Annalen der Physik, and these papers revolutionized physics. One of the revolutionary papers that was on special relativity, Zur Elektrodynamik bewegter Körper, involved electrodynamics of bodies in motion. Another one deduced the formula E=mc2.

In April of 1905, Einstein submitted his dissertation, titled, Eine neue Bestimmung der Moleküldimensionen, which was on molecular dimensions. The University of Zurich accepted the work in July the same year, and in January of the following year, Einstein was awarded his doctorate.

In 1907, Einstein began thinking seriously about General Relativity Theory, and he soon found out the principle of mass-energy equivalence for systems in continual acceleration. He decided to apply for a doctorate at the University of Bern, but he was not successful. He worked on an entirely new dissertation which he handed to the university in 1908, and on its basis the university awarded him the doctorate he wanted. The University of Bern even engaged him as a private lecturer.

In July 1909, Einstein received his very first honorary doctorate degree. It was awarded by the University of Geneva. In October 1909, he left the Patent Office job to become an Associate Professor at the University of Zurich, and in December of the same year he attained membership of the Physikalische Gesellschaft Zurich.

In 1910, the German University in Prague contacted him by phone, and the following year they made him full professor at the university. In November 1910, Einstein attained membership of the Naturforschende Gesellschaft of Zurich.

In October 1911, Einstein took part in the inaugural Solvay Congress held in Brussels. It was in the same year that he calculated light deflection within the sun's gravitational field, leading to his realization that his hypothesis can be proven experimentally by observing the process in during a solar eclipse.

His alma mater, Zurich Polytechnic, invited him in 1912, and he returned to Zurich as a lecturer in August. There, he cooperated with his old-time friend, Marcel Grossman, who had become a Professor of Mathematics at the institution, on the Theory of General Relativity.

Einstein was nominated to join the Prussian Academy of Sciences in 1913, and Max Planck and Walther Nernst were the emissaries who traveled from Berlin to Zurich with the message. Alongside the membership was the post of professor at the university, which did not have teaching obligations, as well as a management post at the Kaiser Wilhelm Institute for Physics which was yet to be established.

Einstein held his very first address at the Prussian Academy on July 2, 1914, and in 1915, he collaborated with J. W. de Haas to perform experimental tests associated with gyromagnetic effect; consequently known as the Einstein-de Haas-effect. He wound up the work he had been doing on the general theory of relativity in November 1915, and then he presented it in form of speech at the Prussian Academy of Sciences. It was a four-part speech. In December of the same year, Einstein is elected to be the Royal Society of Göttingen's corresponding member.

In March 1916, Einstein's article, "The Formal Foundation of the General of Relativity," was published in the Annals of Physics and in May the same year he replaced Max Planck as head of the German Physical Society. He also wound up writing On the Special and General Theory of Relativity, a Popular Account, which is his most famous book. Other important milestone of the year included receiving a call from the Board of Trustees of the Physical-Technical Institute of the German Reich, working on gravitational waves, and reviewing the quantum theory topic.

In 1917, Einstein did some work on cosmology, and in October he also took over leadership of the Kaiser Wilhelm Institute for Physics. He was so happy with the way he was progressing in Berlin that when the University of Zurich, jointly with the Swiss Polytechnic, offered him a job with exemplary terms, he turned it down.

In May 1919, Einstein's forecast in General Relativity Theory, regarding light deflection within the sun's gravitational field, was confirmed by Arthur Stanley Eddington, making Einstein instantly famous, and in November the University of Rostock awarded him an honorary doctorate. Thereafter in April 1920, the Royal

Danish Academy of Sciences and Letters made him a foreign member, and the same year he received a Danish visitor in Berlin, Niels Bohr, who was a physician. In May, Einstein gained membership of Amsterdam's Royal Dutch Academy of Sciences.

Anti-Semitic sentiments were increasingly being expressed against Einstein and affecting the way his relativity theory was being received. There was one particularly acrimonious scientists' meeting at Bad Nauheim in September, with Einstein and the 1905 Nobel Prize winner in Physics, Philipp Lenard, locking horns. Nevertheless, Einstein continued to travel and give lectures. Earlier on in June, he had traveled to Norway and Denmark, and in November he gave an address at the University of Leiden in the Netherlands.

In June 1921, the University of Manchester awarded Einstein an honorary degree as a doctor of science, and in September he gained membership into the Accademia Nazionale dei Lincei in Rom. In April of the following year, he gained membership into the Commission for Intellectual Cooperation, before receiving the Nobel Prize in November. In March 1923, Einstein gained membership into Madrid's Royal Academy of Exact, Physical, and Natural Sciences, and within a couple of days he received an honorary science degree from the University of Madrid.

In the same year, Einstein withdrew from the Commission for Intellectual Cooperation when he realized how ineffective it was. For several years, beginning 1923, Einstein was given membership into various science organizations and honored in different ways across Europe and elsewhere. Even London's Royal Astronomical Society awarded him a gold medal.

In 1938 he worked with Leopold Infeld to publish The Evolution of Physics, and in 1944, work that he had written in 1905 titled, Zur Elektrodynamik bewegter Körper, or On the Electrodynamics of Moved Bodies, fetched six million dollars in an auction held in February in Kansas. In 1949, his autobiographic notes were published, which basically covered his science career as a whole. He had written them in 1946.

Einstein never stopped working on science projects until his death, just as he never abandoned his fight for freedom and justice. Although he is more well-known as a brilliant physicist, the reality is that Einstein touched people in many different spheres of life. The most humbling aspect of this revered man was that even as the world held him in such high esteem, he still remained a humble, and at times, even self-deprecating man.